BACKCOUNTRY ROADS & TRAILS
SAN DIEGO COUNTY

by Jerry Schad

(3rd Edition)

The Touchstone Press
P.O. Box 81
Beaverton, Oregon 97075

Library of Congress
Catalog Card No. 76-57336
I.S.B.N. No. 0-911518-72-X
Copyright© 1977, 1983, 1986, Jerry Schad

contents

area map

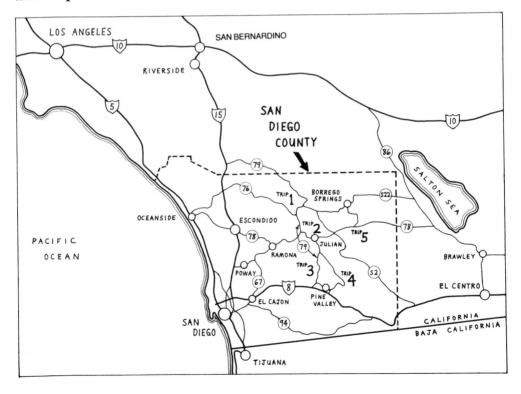

Doane Valley Nature Trail

DISCOVERING
SAN DIEGO COUNTY

San Diego! The mere mention of its name conjures up in the imagination of most people the vision of a subtropical paradise: miles upon miles of sparkling coastline, palm-fringed marinas, and a delightful Mediterranean climate. Surprisingly enough, in addition to these charms, the San Diego resident has within easy driving distance the opportunity to explore another land of surprising contrasts — a world apart — at the expense of a tankful of gasoline or less.

San Diego County is unique: it is blessed with an amazing diversity of climate, terrain and vegetation. Forming its backbone are the Peninsular Ranges, mountains whose rounded summits are crowned with a bountiful growth of conifers. Below and to the east lies some of the rawest kind of desert on earth.

Driving to these back country areas is exciting, but not nearly enough. To fully appreciate the mountain and desert experience, you must abandon your vehicle and strike off on foot into a pine forest or desert wash. Only in this way can you hope to capture the special spirit that each environment has to offer.

Perhaps no other county in the United States can offer so wide a range of recreational activity — year round. Traditionally winter into spring is "the season" for desert buffs, while the mountains attract the greatest number of visitors in the spring and summer. But don't let the "off-seasons" deter you. Experience the bitter wind-whipped chill of a snow-dusted mountain in midwinter, or the fury of the sun and desiccating heat of a midsummer's day in the desert. At these times in particular you may find peace and solitude — qualities that are difficult to find anywhere, let alone close by.

This book is designed primarily with the hiking enthusiast in mind. It is divided into five specific trip sections: the first four are mountain areas within one or two hours driving time from San Diego; while the fifth, the Anza-Borrego Desert in the eastern part of the county, requires about two hours one-way. For each trip you will find a listing of campgrounds, picnic grounds, and points of interest, as well as information on the paved highways leading into the area. Following this data is a detailed description of selected trails.

The majority of the walks in this book are short and easy enough for the whole family to enjoy, with the exception of a few that are suitable for extended day hikes or overnight backpacking. Adverse weather conditions (heavy snow in winter or excessive heat in summer) could prevent exploration of some of the longer trails, but good climate is likely to prevail most of the year. Special mountain-climbing skills are not required, but a moderate amount of physical conditioning is desirable.

Perhaps the most important aspect is that of preparation. Preparedness can make the difference between a pleasant experience on the trail and one which could prove to be, at best, miserable. These few suggestions may help:

1) Adequate clothing and footwear.

This includes warm clothing on cold days in the mountains. Temperatures may drop to below freezing, and strong winds are common in exposed areas. Remember to keep extremities warm. A cap and mittens should suffice for this. Desert hiking on warm days may actually require more clothing than you might expect. Loose fitting, light-colored clothes with adequate ventilation provide protection from the sun. A sun hat is essential, while long pants are helpful in the event of a painful encounter with cactus spines. Lightweight but sturdy hiking boots are ideal for all trails in this book, but running shoes are adequate for the less rocky trails.

2) A sufficient amount of water and nourishment.

Water is generally not available along the trails, and many walks traverse very arid regions. It is absolutely essential to carry a canteen on desert walks. Quick energy snacks and the like are useful to stave off fatigue on the longer hikes.

View from Culp Valley

3) A good psychological attitude.

This comes naturally to a child, but the adult city-dweller may find it difficult to reorient himself to an entirely different sensory viewpoint. Rewards are many for those who are open-eyed, open-eared, and open minded.

Remember the backpacker's motto: "Take only memories, leave only footprints." Not everyone lives up to this ideal, and you may add to the enjoyment of those who follow by helping to remove and pack out any trash that has been thoughtlessly discarded by others.

The mountains of Southern California are especially vulnerable to destructive wildfires. For this reason, do not smoke or build fires on the trails.

Visitors to the Anza-Borrego Desert State Park must observe rules that are designed to protect its fragile environment and natural beauty. Ecologists estimate that it takes 500 years for nature to restore a given area to its original condition, once it has been denuded of vegetation; and with a million park visitors per year, it is easy to imagine the damage that could result without the existence and enforcement of these regulations:

Vehicles must be driven only on approved routes of travel. Ground fires are prohibited, and desert vegetation, whether dead or alive, may never be used for fuel. No animal, plant or mineral may be collected and removed from the park. And finally, pets must be kept on leash at all times.

Archeological sites and Indian petroglyphs are also protected by law. Disturbing these sites is a serious offense. Vandalism and theft at petroglyph sites is reaching intolerable proportions; unless it ceases, a valuable portion of ancient Native American heritage will be lost.

Aside from taking a few simple precautions and observing the special regulations, a day spent hiking in the mountains or deserts of San Diego County is little more trouble than a day's visit to the beach or Balboa Park. But a walk in the backcountry wilderness adds up to much more than just a diversion, an escape from the dizzy, endless cycle of urban-style living. It is a chance to get back to the roots, those ultimate realities that are too often forgotten by older generations and yet-to-be-discovered by younger generations. It is a moment of freedom, a time of renewal and self-discovery.

This, then, is an invitation to the wonders that lie only a short distance away. Come explore this land, and learn to appreciate its many moods. Above all, treat it lovingly and with respect, for this is the key to its preservation for generations yet unborn.

Mendenhall Valley Overlook

THE MOUNTAIN EXPERIENCE

For many persons a trip to the mountains of San Diego County consists of a drive to the Palomar Mountains for a look at the 200-inch telescope, or perhaps to Julian to pick up a box of apples or a jug of cider. While this approach certainly cannot be faulted, it is nevertheless difficult to appreciate the true charms of the mountain country from the roadside alone. People do come here with the intention of exploring our mountains on foot; even so, existence of easily accessible trails leading to remote and beautiful backcountry is not usually advertised. Many visitors who are aware of the existence of these trails and at the same time willing and capable hikers, are reluctant to try them if they have already tackled the John Muir Trail or conquered Half Dome in Yosemite National Park. Surely the mountains of San Diego County would be a letdown in comparison to the majestic Sierra Nevada or similar ranges to the north. This attitude may be justified to a certain extent, but there are surprises in San Diego County, too, awaiting even the most seasoned hiker. Some areas, notably the Palomar and Cuyamaca Mountains, exhibit characteristics of terrain and vegetation that are remarkably similar to the mid-elevation western slopes of the Sierra Nevada; one area in particular, the Laguna Mountains, offers vertical relief and contrasts rivaling other well-known massive fault scarps such as the east slopes of the Sierra Nevada and the San Jacinto Mountains.

Whatever the virtues of our mountains compared to others, they do offer a chance

to get away from it all with a minimum of travel commitment. Many of the trails included in this section are within an hour's drive of metropolitan San Diego. In addition, our mountains boast an acceptable — if not ideal — climate year-round.

Why should one choose to spend his leisure time hiking in the mountains rather than visiting one of the amusement spots for which Southern California is justly famous? As an individual, the rewards are these: the feeling of physical satisfaction — healthy fatigue — after a day's hike; the opportunity to open the senses to the subtle, yet fundamental workings of the natural world. As part of a group of family or friends, the hiker can share these experiences and thus enhance them.

A walk through the woods can provide the sensitive observer with vivid images of the universal life and death cycle of all things animate and inanimate — from geological formations acted upon by erosive forces, to minutiae such as the inner workings of a colony of ants. Colors, shapes, scents and sounds can take on new meanings. Even a small, seemingly insignificant event as a leaf falling gently on a fresh autumn breeze can become a moment to be treasured forever.

The four mountain areas I have chosen for this book combine the best of desirable features for the day hiker. All walks in this section are on public property — either a state or county park, or within the boundaries of the Cleveland National Forest.

Geologically the mountains of San Diego County are part of the Peninsular Ranges, so-named because they form the backbone of the Baja California peninsula. The extension of these ranges intrudes some 130 miles into the State of California, with the Santa Ana Mountains in Orange County and San Jacinto Mountains in Riverside County marking the northern limit. Major components in San Diego County include the forested Agua Tibia and Palomar Mountains, the Cuyamaca Mountains, and the Laguna Mountains, all of which are included in this section (trips 1-4). Desert ranges of the county, such as the Santa Rosa Mountains and Vallecito Mountains, are also part of the Peninsular Range;

and hikes in these areas are treated in the desert section (trips) of this book.

In the wetter coastal portions of the Peninsular Ranges, west—facing foothills are covered with dense chaparral. Then at higher elevations of up to four or five thousand feet oak trees make their appearance. If not burned over by forest fires, most territory above 5,000 feet is forested. Pines, firs, and cedars, intermixed with deciduous trees, are typically found here, alternating with open meadows on the moderate or flat terrain. East-facing slopes tend to be steep and desert-like. Chaparral thins out rapidly toward lower elevations, and abrupt contrasts in topography and vegetation may be seen along the edge of some of these slopes, notably the Laguna Mountain crest along Sunrise Highway.

A wide variety of wildlife exists today in the mountains as it always has. Natives of the middle and upper elevations include southern mule deer, raccoons, squirrels, gray foxes, striped and spotted skunks, and many species of birds. Predators, such as coyotes, bobcats, and even mountain lions, are somewhat common, but discreet.

Human population in the mountains of San Diego County is thinly distributed. Several thousand people, however, do reside in and around the Julian area, where a large portion of the acreage is privately owned. Julian has seen its heyday as a gold-boom town in the last century, and today has a peaceful existence as an apple growing center. The remainder of the mountainous territory in San Diego County is devoted for the most part to ranching, or has been left in a pristine state for the benefit of all.

After a while the allure of mountain pines and clear blue skies beckons even the most seasoned city-dweller. So follow your inclinations and head for the mountains soon, and enjoy!

area map – Palomar Mountains

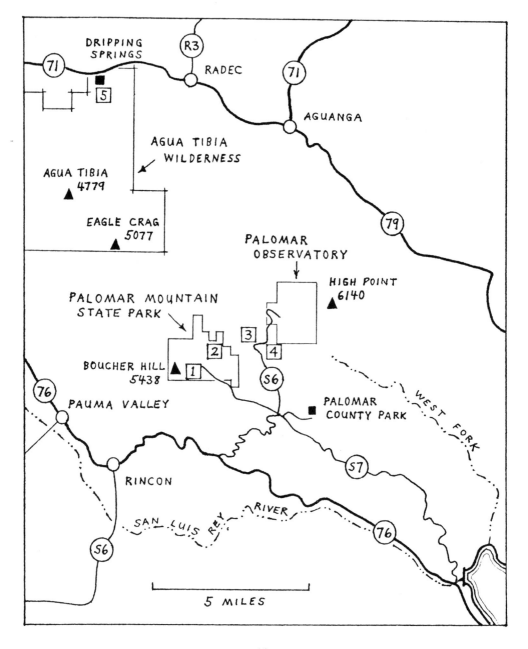

Trip 1 • The Palomar Mountains

Points of Interest: Palomar Observatory

Campgrounds: Cedar Grove and Doane Valley Campgrounds at Palomar Mountain State Park. Fry Creek and Observatory Campgrounds near Palomar Observatory, La Jolla Indian Reservation Campground on Highway 76, Dripping Springs campground on Highway 79 (Riverside County), Palomar County Park

Picnic Grounds: Silver Crest Picnic Area in Palomar Mountain State Park, Fry Creek and Observatory Campgrounds, San Luis Rey Picnic Ground on Highway 76

The Palomar Mountain region holds a special fascination. Not only is this the most magnificently wooded area in all of San Diego County, but it also cradles atop its highlands one of the most important astronomical observatories in the world. The 200-inch Hale telescope at Palomar Observatory, the nation's largest, has done more to increase man's understanding of the universe than any other such instrument.

The Palomar Mountains, if they may be called such, are actually made up of several mountain ridges. The major ones are Palomar Mountain itself, on which the observatory is located; Aguanga Mountain, east of the observatory; and Agua Tibia Mountain, on the western end of the group. The point of highest elevation, on Palomar Mountain, is unimaginatively dubbed "High Point." The observatory itself is located about two miles west of High Point in a clearing on a flat-topped ridge of solid granite covered by top soil.

Historically, the Palomar Mountains were occupied by Indian tribes long before the coming of the white man. Bedrock mortar holes in the granite of the mountain indicate the existence of inhabitants who relied heavily upon the production of acorn food products. These early mountain dwellers called the area "Paauw," a Shoshonean Indian word meaning "pigeon roost." Band-tailed pigeons once nested on the slopes, and today many of these birds remain on the mountain year-round.

Thousands of acres of well-wooded uplands and gentle valleys in the Palomar Mountain region are within the jurisdiction of the Cleveland National Forest or the California Department of Parks and Recreation. A large portion of the south facing slope, however, is under private ownership. The dry, brushy north slopes, including the Agua Tibia Wilderness, have in the past been subject to seasonal fire closures during which all entry is prohibited. The closing of this fire-susceptible area during the most hazardous periods has undoubtedly helped to protect it during critical periods. In contrast to similar areas in San Diego County, the Cuyamaca and Laguna Mountains for example, the upper-elevation forests of the Palomar Mountains have been preserved to a remarkable degree.

In many parts of these mountains, the delightful mixture of large pines, firs and cedars intermixed with live oaks and black oaks suggest a Sierra Nevada atmosphere. Stands of virgin chaparral, unburned for more than a century, may be found in the Agua Tibia Wilderness Area.

For all the beauty and popularity of the Palomar Mountains, relatively few trails are found here. Those that do exist, however, penetrate the most inspiring portions of the mountain. Trails in the Palomar Mountain State Park and Fry Creek-Observatory Campground area of the Cleveland National Forest, as well as the Dripping Springs Trail leading into the Agua Tibia Wilderness, are included in the following sections.

The nearly two-hour drive from San Diego to Palomar is a pleasant one. The quickest and most direct route takes you north on Interstate 15 to County Highway S6 in Escondido. Simply follow S6 some 30 miles northeast to the Palomar Mountain summits. For a few miles S6 joins with California Highway 76, then later splits off to climb stiffly up the slopes. Fragrant citrus and dark avocado groves flank Highway 76 until it begins to climb upward from the flatlands. Two alternatives are available here: you may continue on S6 forking to the left at South Grade Road (also known as Highway to the Stars), or you may continue eastward on 76 to East Grade Road (County S7) at Lake Henshaw. Both South Grade and East Grade lead to your destination, but the former is a steep, winding ascent, while the latter offers a gentle, but longer, approach. At the top of the mountain, East Grade Road continues to Palomar Mountain State Park, while S6 runs past the National Forest campgrounds to the observatory. A store and cafe will be found at this intersection.

On the way up, you may be fortunate to witness the daring descent of a hang-gliding enthusiast. The spectacular dropoffs along East Grade Road feature a steady updraft — ideal conditions for a long ride. The nearly 3000-foot descent from East Grade to the valley below (near Highway 76) takes only about ten minutes. Surely nothing can be so terrifying and exhilarating as actually flying off the top of a mountain on a kite!

From the north county communities, you may take Highway 76, which follows the San Luis Rey River east from Oceanside. If returning via East Grade Road, San Diego-bound motorists may elect to take Highways 76 and 79 south from Lake Henshaw to Santa Ysabel; then Highway 78 west to Ramona; thence to San Diego via Highway 67. Whatever route you choose, you will undoubtedly enjoy a pleasant diversion through the San Diego backcountry.

Along Doane Creek

Upper Doane Valley

Trip 1, Trail 1 ● Palomar Mountain State Park: Scott's Cabin to Boucher Hill

Approximate distance: 3.5 miles round trip
Elevation at trailhead: 5,220 feet
Low point (Cedar Grove Campground):
  4,840 feet
High point (Boucher Hill): 5,420 feet

The Sierra Nevada-like atmosphere of Palomar Mountain State Park makes it a perfect retreat — even if only for a day. Overlooking a large part of Southern California from a mile-high altitude, the park consists of nearly 2,000 acres of rolling timberland interspersed with gentle meadowland and deeply shaded ravines. A small network of paved roads and trails runs throughout the park, affording ample opportunity for leisurely exploration by car or on foot.

One possible trail loop begins near park headquarters and includes a visit to the ruins of Scott's Cabin and a view of the lowlands from Boucher Hill. Park in the large lot at Silver Crest Picnic Area and Observation

Point, then pick up the trail across the road. Not much remains of the log cabin which was built by the little known homesteader who was believed to have tended the old apple orchard at the entrance to the park. From Scott's Cabin the trail heads sharply downhill to Cedar Grove Campground. The Adams Trail, which is next, begins on the far side of the campground. I found it to be the most delightful part of the walk, particularly since a freak summer thunderstorm had just arrived and left the dogwood and leopard lilies glistening.

Adams Trail winds steadily uphill through the thick undergrowth in the shadows of the trees, and at one point crosses a small ravine. It becomes Boucher Trail after crossing Nate Harrison Road.

The high point of the hike (and the park) is Boucher Hill, which is topped by a fire lookout. If scenic possibilities are taken into account, the return to park headquarters is best made by the paved road on the south side of Boucher Hill.

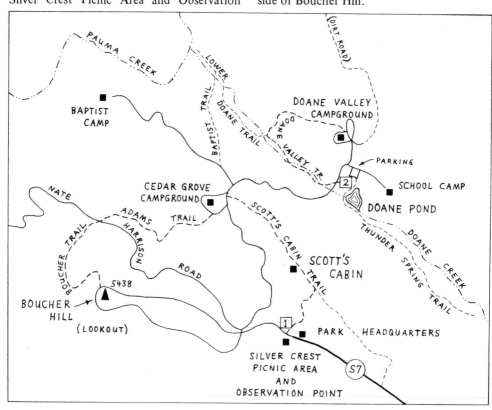

Trip 1, Trail 2 • Palomar Mountain State Park: Doane Valley Nature Trail

Approximate distance: **1.0 mile round trip**
Elevation at trailhead: **4,660 feet**
Low point: **4,550 feet**
High point: **4,700 feet**

Nowhere else in the county, in my opinion, will you find comparable mountain scenery and atmosphere to match the forests and meadows along Doane Creek. The Doane Valley Nature Trail, a loop through Lower Doane Valley, offers the best in scenic possibilities. A highly informative trail guide leaflet may be obtained at the trailhead, with descriptions of the wide variety of vegetation along the trail.

The box containing trail guides is in the parking lot adjacent to Doane Pond. The lake is stocked with trout, and is open to fishing year-round. Picnic tables with stoves are here, as well as rest rooms. Walking downstream along Doane Creek, when it is flowing in the early part of the year, is a genuine delight. Lining the creek are magnificent white fir, incense cedar, box elder and white alder trees, all described in detail by the leaflet. Lower Doane Meadow begins rather abruptly. Late spring and early summer wildflowers splash color across the rolling expanse of park-like meadow, and mature specimens of pine, fir and cedar form an imposing wall surrounding it. Lower Doane Trail, branching to the left, will take you to Pauma Creek if you wish to make the side trip. The nature trail itself continues back uphill to Doane Valley Campground which is a few hundred yards by paved road from the starting point at Doane Pond.

On Pauma Creek

Trip 1, Trail 3 • Fry Creek Nature Trail

Approximate distance: 1.0 mile (1 way)
Low point (trailhead): 4,930 feet
High point (Penny Pines): 5,300 feet

This short walk along the heavily wooded slopes overlooking Fry Creek is best experienced in the month of October. The eye is simply delighted by the contrasting blue of the sky, somber green of the live oak and pine, and traditional yellow and orange autumn color of the black oak. The weather is changeable this time of year — warm Indian summer days alternate with crisp wintry periods, but clear skies are likely to prevail. Autumn is a time when the slightest breeze may unleash a torrent of falling acorns, and squirrels scurry about gathering a harvest to last the winter.

The trail begins at the entrance to Fry Creek Campground, off County Highway S6, and ends in a Penny Pines plantation at the upper end of the Fry Creek drainage. There are two ways to return: retrace your path on the nature trail, or take the dirt road to the left past the pines plantation (which later becomes a paved road) for a quick descent through the camping and picnic area along the banks of the creek.

Acorn Cache

18

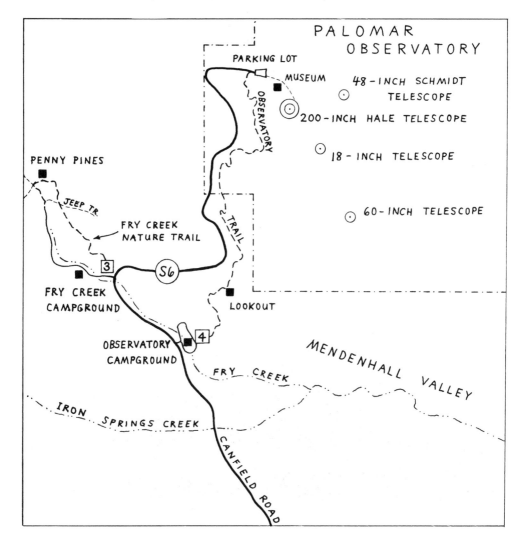

PALOMAR
OBSERVATORY

PARKING LOT

MUSEUM

48-INCH SCHMIDT
TELESCOPE

200-INCH HALE TELESCOPE

OBSERVATORY

18-INCH TELESCOPE

PENNY PINES

60-INCH TELESCOPE

JEEP TR

FRY CREEK
NATURE TRAIL

TRAIL

3

S6

FRY CREEK
CAMPGROUND

LOOKOUT

4

OBSERVATORY
CAMPGROUND

FRY CREEK

MENDENHALL VALLEY

IRON SPRINGS CREEK

CANFIELD ROAD

Trip 1, Trail 4 • Observatory Trail

Approximate distance: 2.0 miles (1 way)
Low point (Observatory Campground):
4,770 feet
High point (Palomar Observatory): 5,570
feet

As would be expected, the average tourist visitor to Palomar Observatory arrives in an automobile via the paved road, takes in the sights, and departs in a like fashion. Few are aware of the trail that roughly parallels the final two miles of road, beginning at Observatory Campground. It offers a great deal of flexibility for a day's outing: a family might decide to picnic at the campground, then spend the afternoon hiking to the observatory and returning by the same trail. Or a one-way trip either direction could be arranged by members of a group if transportation is available through others. The ascent to the observatory from the campground involves an 800-foot elevation gain, so less athletically inclined persons might wish to make only the descent.

Benches are provided at convenient intervals along the trail for those who wish to rest. One resting spot looks out over Mendenhall Valley. The tributary creeks entering the valley from the surrounding woodland comprise the headwaters of the west fork of the San Luis Rey River. Downstream, the waters pass through the partially flooded Lake Henshaw basin, and flow eastward alongside the present route of Highway 76.

The first sight of the 200-inch Hale telescope dome, appearing as an irridescent hemisphere towering over the trees, is quite startling. But the enormous scale of the building and the instrument inside is not fully realized until seen from the viewing gallery inside. A museum nearby exhibits photographs of astronomical objects taken with Palomar Observatory telescopes, and contains a scale model of the 200-inch diameter mirror. Visitors are welcome from 8 a.m. to 5 p.m. daily.

Palomar Observatory

Trip 1, Trail 5 ● Agua Tibia Wilderness: Dripping Springs Trail

Approximate distance: 6.5 miles (1 way)
Low point (trailhead): 1,630 feet
High point (end of trail): 4,420 feet

Wilderness areas have been set aside by the Forest Service to protect special areas in the state that have remained essentially untouched since the coming of the white man. Agua Tibia Wilderness in the Palomar Mountains is the first such reserve in San Diego County. Of special interest here are the stands of native chaparral that have not been burned over for at least 100 years.

While the upper elevations of Agua Tibia Mountain are contained in San Diego County, its chaparral-clad lower slopes extend northward into Riverside County. Dripping Springs Trail begins in Riverside County at Dripping Springs Campground and ascends 2,800 feet to the pines near the summit of the mountain. The round trip completion of the entire trip in one day can be considered a challenge to all but the most physically fit individuals, but even less-motivated hikers should find the lower end of the trail interesting.

To reach the trailhead from San Diego, drive north on Interstate 15, then 10 miles east on Highway 79 to Dripping Springs Campground. In order to obtain the required wilderness permit for entrance into the area, stop at the Forest Service station at the entrance to the campground. The area may be closed from July 1 to the end of the fire season in autumn, so check with the Forest Service beforehand if in doubt.

Just beyond the campground, Dripping Springs Trail crosses the boulder-strewn bed of Arroyo Seco Creek, then immediately begins the switchback ascent. Vail Lake, with a backdrop of Southern California's loftiest mountains, comes into view in the north. Low shrubs eventually give way to larger specimens, then finally to giant chaparral. Ordinarily, periodic fires sweep across the tinder-dry hillsides of Southern California, discouraging the survival of mature chaparral. But here you will find examples of truly gargantuan-sized shrubs — manzanita and red shanks — grown to heights of 20 feet.

After four miles the trail descends a little and a view opens up to the southeast. The white dome of the Hale Telescope at Palomar Observatory gleams on a distant ridge. Soon you follow sharp switchbacks again, with the scenery changing from chaparral to oak and pine this time. At trail's end is the Magee-Palomar Trail, an abandoned fire road maintained only as a foot trail. For a fine view of the mountains and valleys to the south and the Pacific Ocean in the west, walk a few hundred feet southeast on the Magee-Palomar Trail to a point overlooking Castro Canyon.

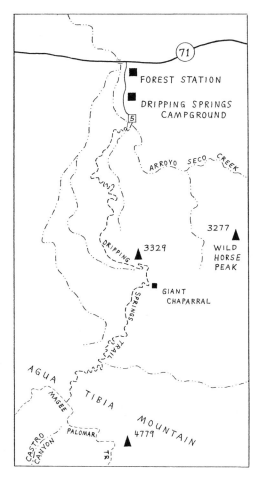

area map – Julian, Cuyamaca Mountains, Laguna Mountains

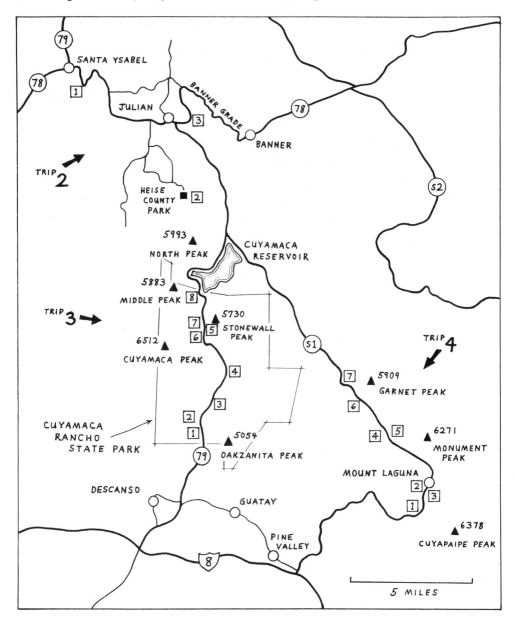

Backcountry road near Julian

Trip 2 • The Julian Area

Points of Interest: Julian Museum, Eagle Mine

Campgrounds: William Heise County Park

Picnic Grounds: Inaja Memorial Picnic Ground and William Heise County Park

On the first of March, 1870, nine days after the discovery of a gold-bearing quartz ledge in the pine-covered mountains behind San Diego, a shipment of 1,200 pounds of rich ore arrived in the city, where one-third of it was dumped into a store window downtown for public exhibition. Crowds gathered and excitement grew by the minute. A horde of would-be prospectors grabbed what implements were available and hastened to stake their own claim to wealth in the mountains. The stampede was on. When they arrived at the gold mines, the hopes of the miners were inflamed by the discovery of a new strike nearby, and another the following day, and yet another . . .

In the first month of frantic activity, 260 claims and 40 noteworthy discoveries were made. One miner wrote in the San Diego Daily Union: "One scarcely knows whether he is on his head or heels. Imagine 800 men turned loose in the mountains with as little sense and as much 'friskyness' as many wild horses. The people here are positively wild. Such a thing as sober thought is unknown. The rumor comes that Tom, Dick, or Harry has struck it, and forthwith the whole camp rushes pell-mell for the new diggin's. People don't sleep here at all, or if they do, they are more lucky than I."

A mining district was organized and named after Mike S. Julian, a pioneer settler and former Confederate captain. The townsite was hastily laid out and lots surveyed by "stepping them off." By 1872, gold shipments from the Julian-Banner-Wynola area were averaging $9,000 a week, and the Stonewall Mine near Cuyamaca Lake was well on its way to producing an eventual $2,000,000 worth of gold.

Gold mining began to decline in 1874 with the exhaustion of easily milled ore. Big strikes elsewhere were luring miners away, and other men turned to ranching or agriculture. Except for a brief resurgence of activity in the 1890's, the gold rush had ended by the 1880's. The legacy of Julian in the twentieth century had become not that of gold, but of apples. In 1915, the Julian apple exhibit at the San Francisco World's Fair took the Gold Cup in its class, and today as then the residents of Julian pride themselves on the superior quality of their apples. Some years, the townspeople hold an apple festival to celebrate the fall harvests. This convivial gathering usually attracts so many visitors from all over the state that the town has been literally overwhelmed on past occasions.

Today the town of Julian, set amid the gentle farmland and forests surrounding it, scarcely betrays the turmoil of its early existence. Tool into town on Main Street, and the old-fashioned storefront facades seem to strike a pose reminiscent of similar sleepy towns in the Mother Lode country of Northern California. Just around the corner, on the road to Santa Ysabel, is the Julian Museum (open Saturdays, Sundays and holidays) which contains tools, clothing, home furnishings, and other artifacts of the gold rush days. Nearby you may tour the Eagle Mine, a restored working gold mine. Drive out C Street, north of town, to reach the entrance.

Seven miles west of Julian, on Highway 78/79, is Santa Ysabel. Long before the arrival of the gold miners, an "asistencia" or sub-mission was established here by the padres from Mission San Diego to handle the many Indians who lived on the mountain rancherias. Today a new chapel stands upon the old site, and continues to serve the Indians of several reservations in the vicinity.

To fully capture the country atmosphere of the Julian area, you should drive or bicycle the back roads which ramble over the rolling hills, across the orchards, and through the wooded ravines in back of town. Farmer Road and Wynola Road (north of town); and Pine Hills Road, Eagle Peak Road, Deer Lake Park Road, and Frisius Drive (south of town) are all excellent for this purpose. William Heise County Park is the place to go for a picnic and some casual hiking.

In selecting a route to Julian, San Diegans have a choice between two basic routes, each 60 miles in length. It's convenient then, for the sake of variety, to make this a loop trip instead of an up and back drive. From San Diego you may proceed east on Interstate 8 to Descanso, then go north on Highway 79 through Cuyamaca Rancho State Park to Julian. Or alternately you may travel Highway 78 through Ramona and Santa Ysabel to Julian. Ramona is reached from San Diego via Interstate 15, Poway Road (Highway S4), and Highway 67; or from El Cajon via Highway 67.

While in the Julian area, stop at one of the many friendly roadside markets or fruitstands. You might wish to try a cup of hot or ice-cold apple cider, depending on the season, or purchase some of the locally grown fruit or vegetables to take home with you.

Along Main Street – Julian

Trip 2, Trail 1 • Inaja Trail

Approximate distance: 1.0 mile round trip
Low point (trailhead): 3,320 feet
High point: 3,440 feet

The Inaja Trail is a short loop originating at Inaja Memorial Picnic Ground, located just one mile from Santa Ysabel and six miles from Julian on Highway 78/79. It is worth it to stop here briefly and climb the knoll overlooking the headwaters of the San Diego River. At the top of the trail you will come upon a direction finder which may be used to point out the major landmarks of the area. Occasionally, on spring and summer mornings, you may find that the coastal fog layer has hidden all but the tops of the ridges and peaks around you. From the north side of the trail there is a view of the fertile Santa Ysabel Valley with its backdrop of oak-studded, rolling hills.

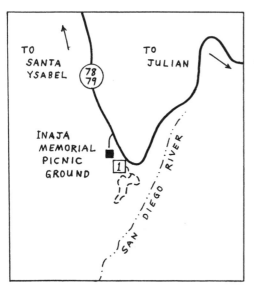

Inaja Trail

26

Trip 2, Trail 2 • William Heise County Park

Approximate distances: 1.0 mile round trip (nature trail), 2.0 miles round trip (wilderness hike)
Low point (trailhead): 4,100 feet
High point on "wilderness hike": 4,320 feet

In contrast to most other parks in the extensive San Diego County system, William Heise Park is large enough to support a modest network of hiking trails. Set among majestic live oaks in a secluded valley at about 4,000 feet, it is available for day use without charge every day of the year. Drive one mile west from Julian to Pine Hills Road, then follow the signs to the entrance to the park.

Once inside, proceed to the picnic area in the westernmost corner of the park, where you can pick up the one-mile self-guided nature trail. When the nature trail loops back to the picnic area, stay on the right fork if you wish to include the wilderness hike. This trail adds another two miles of distance if you take the longest loop. Breaking out of the trees, the wilderness hike ascends the dense chaparral slopes overlooking the park. Most impressive are the fine stands of manzanita — a shrub characterized by smooth, reddish limbs. Views of the Cuyamaca Mountains are also furnished in several places along the trail.

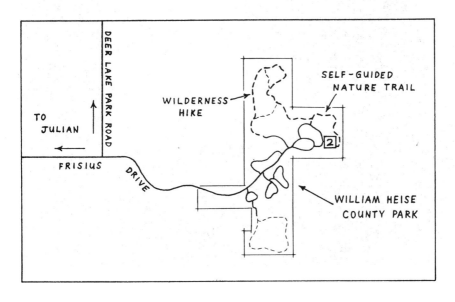

27

Warlock Mine ruins

Trip 2, Trail 3 ● Old Banner Grade

Approximate distance: 1.5 miles (1 way)
Low point (Warlock Mine Group): 3,460 feet
High point (trailhead): 4,160 feet

Gold mining in San Diego County has all but ceased, but the traces remain. For a look at some of the more recently abandoned prospects around Julian, take a walk down the old Banner Grade.

Drive about one mile east of Julian on Highway 78, then make a right turn at Whispering Pines Road. Immediately after, make another sharp right to connect with Woodland Road. One half mile beyond, take the left fork and park off the road at the locked gate. From here you may proceed on foot on what is actually the old Banner Grade route.

Down below is the modern road through Banner Canyon – Highway 78. It appears only slightly less twisting than the old road, but offers a more gradual, if longer, descent to the town of Banner. Abandoned mine shafts pierce the earth on the steep slopes above and below you, but many of them have been concealed by brush. The Warlock Mine Group, including a processing mill, comes into view about one mile from the gate. In operation as late as the 1950's, the site has now been reduced to dilapidated ruins.

Beyond the Warlock Group, old Banner Grade runs into private property, so it is best to turn back at this point. Not surprisingly, the return trip of 700 feet elevation gain will take considerably longer than the deceptively easy descent to the mines.

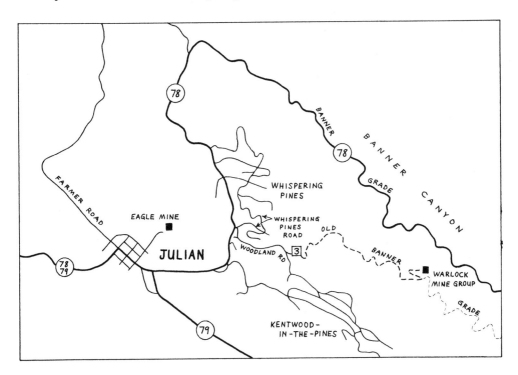

area map – Julian, Cuyamaca Mountains, Laguna Mountains

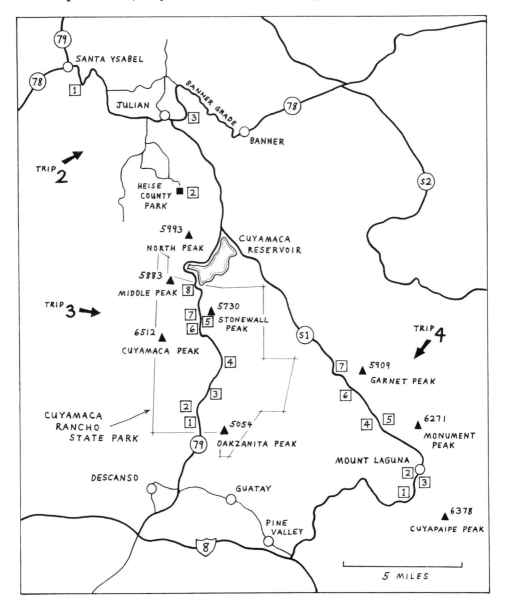

SANTA YSABEL

79

78

1

JULIAN

BANNER GRADE

3

78

BANNER

TRIP 2

HEISE COUNTY PARK

2

S2

5993 ▲
NORTH PEAK

CUYAMACA RESERVOIR

5883 ▲
MIDDLE PEAK

8

TRIP 3 →

7

5730 ▲
5   STONEWALL PEAK

6

6512 ▲
CUYAMACA PEAK

TRIP 4

S1

4

7

5909 ▲
GARNET PEAK

3

6

CUYAMACA RANCHO STATE PARK

2

1

79

5054 ▲
OAKZANITA PEAK

4   5

6271 ▲
MONUMENT PEAK

MOUNT LAGUNA

2

3

DESCANSO

GUATAY

1

PINE VALLEY

8

6378 ▲
CUYAPAIPE PEAK

5 MILES

30

Dry lake bed – Cuyamaca Lake

Trip 3 • The Cuyamaca Mountains

Points of Interest: Indian exhibit at Cuyamaca Rancho State Park headquarters, natural history exhibit at Paso Picacho Campground, Stonewall Mine ruins

Campgrounds: Paso Picacho Campground and Green Valley Campground in Cuyamaca Rancho State Park

Picnic Grounds: At Paso Picacho and Green Valley Campgrounds

The Cuyamaca Mountains are literally in the backyard of San Diego, and this proximity serves to enhance the contrasts between these two areas. The heavily populated coastal plain and foothills teem with the hustle and bustle of man's modern-day style of living, while in the mountains Nature is clearly master of its domain. Lacking the gentle ocean-moderated climate of the coastal strip, but possessing a larger than usual share of rainfall, the mountains experience the full four seasons and a perpetually blue sky.

Having the Cuyamaca Mountain area close at hand is beneficial in that most of it is contained within Cuyamaca Rancho State Park, and thus readily available to the public. Well-developed visitor facilities, in addition to a state highway through the park, have made these mountains a popular retreat in any season.

The Cuyamaca Mountains have, in fact, always been a favorite of Southern California inhabitants. As early as 7,000 years ago and until as recently as the gold boom of 1870, the Cuyamacas were a summer residence of the Kumeyaay Indians. Even the name Cuyamaca derives from a Spanish version of the Indian word meaning approximately "the place where it rains."

In 1845, the park area was incorporated into Rancho Cuyamaca by the Mexican government, and subsequently it changed hands several times until its eventual purchase by the State of California in 1933.

Taking into consideration sheer beauty and delightful climate, the best seasons to visit are, in my opinion, spring and autumn.

The summer and winter seasons do have their highlights, though. An occasional thunderstorm may temper a warm, dry day of late summer, and bring out the earthy aroma of forest or chaparral. During a winter of heavy precipitation, a foot or two of snow may accumulate on the higher peaks and ridges; and sometimes, after a passing storm, the air may remain exceptionally clear for a day or two. The virtues of spring and fall need not be elaborated — anyone who has lived in a four-seasons climate will understand.

The diversity of terrain and plant life in the Cuyamaca Mountains supports an abundance of wildlife. One example of this is the wide variety of birds found in the area. Located midway between the coast and desert, it is attractive to many species normally associated with coastal or desert environments. The natural history exhibit at Paso Picacho Campground is worth visiting if you intend to explore the park on foot.

Tranquillity may be found here, off the highway, on the more than 100 miles of hiking and equestrian trails throughout the park. Two primitive camps for backpackers, Arroyo Seco and Granite Springs, are located near the outer boundaries; two horsemen's facilities are at the north end of the park. By and large, however, the trail system is best suited to one-day exploration, and I have described in the following sections only some of the more interesting trails suitable for day hikes.

From San Diego, the Cuyamaca Mountains may be reached within an hour by way of Interstate 8. Simply drive east on I-8, taking the Highway 79 exit north. In Descanso Valley, two prominent features of the area, Cuyamaca Peak and Stonewall Peak, come into view. Cuyamaca's rounded summit marks the highest point within 30 miles. Stonewall Peak, to the right of Cuyamaca Peak, is nearly 1,000 feet lower, but its pointed, rocky summit is distinctive compared to its neighbors. There are several turnouts on Highway 79 between Green Valley and Paso Picacho Campgrounds. Free parking is allowed here during the day, as well as at park headquarters. Overnight parking is prohibited. A small day use fee is charged, as is a more substantial overnight camping fee for the use of the facilities at the campgrounds, and many of the trails originate from these points.

Highway 79 crests at Paso Picacho Campground, located at the low point of the saddle connecting Stonewall Peak and Cuyamaca Peak. The two most spectacular trails, to Cuyamaca and Stonewall, begin here, and heavy use attests to their popularity.

Near the north end of the park, a paved road branches to the right. This provides access to the horsemen's camps and leads to the Stonewall Mine near Cuyamaca Reservoir. The mine was the most productive of the Julian-area gold boom, and to this day old mining relics may be seen on the site. Nearby, the town of Cuyamaca had grown up to serve the sudden influx of population.

Leaving the park, Highway 79 encircles Cuyamaca Reservoir and finally heads north to Julian. The water level of the lake is usually kept low, but it is possible to rent a boat or fish here. A cafe and store are conveniently located along the highway.

You may enjoy returning to San Diego by an alternate route. Take Highway 79 north to Julian, then go west on Highway 78 through Santa Ysabel. At Ramona, Highway 78 continues toward Escondido and Oceanside, while Highway 67 runs south to El Cajon and San Diego.

Near Paso Picacho Campground

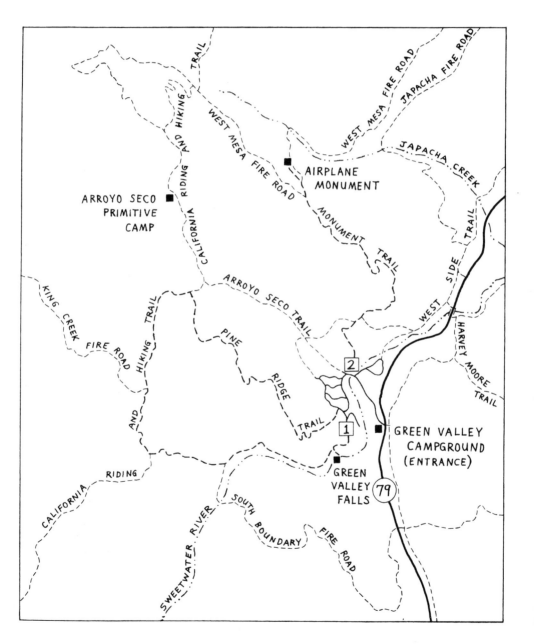

WEST MESA FIRE ROAD

JAPACHA FIRE ROAD

AND HIKING TRAIL

WEST MESA FIRE ROAD

WEST MESA FIRE ROAD

JAPACHA CREEK

CALIFORNIA RIDING

AIRPLANE
MONUMENT

ARROYO SECO
PRIMITIVE
CAMP

MONUMENT TRAIL

ARROYO SECO TRAIL

WEST SIDE TRAIL

KING CREEK FIRE ROAD

AND HIKING TRAIL

PINE

RIDGE

HARVEY MOORE TRAIL

2

1

TRAIL

GREEN VALLEY
CAMPGROUND
(ENTRANCE)

CALIFORNIA

RIDING

GREEN
VALLEY
FALLS

79

SWEETWATER RIVER

SOUTH BOUNDARY

FIRE ROAD

Trip 3, Trail 1 • Green Valley Falls — Pine Ridge Trail

Approximate distance: 4.0 miles round trip
Low point (Green Valley Falls): 3,850 feet
High point (Pine Ridge): 4,400 feet

The Green Valley Campground is set among a magnificent stand of canyon live oak and ponderosa pine at the southern end of Green Valley. Nearby the Sweetwater River narrows and cascades over a series of falls. This is the best area to begin a hike through the dry chaparral slopes of the southwestern corner of Cuyamaca Rancho State Park. The most convenient place to start is the Falls Picnic Area at the southern end of the campground.

Follow the jeep road marked "Falls Trail." Shortly beyond, a spur trail to the left leads to Green Valley Falls. Rather pretentious in its name, the falls are actually a mere trickle most of the time except for periods of heavy precipitation. On quiet days, the reflecting pools trapped in the rocks mirror the surrounding trees, creating a memorable scene.

Return to the jeep trail, and continue in the downstream direction. At the next intersection take South Boundary Fire Road uphill to the California Riding and Hiking Trail. The vegetation changes from pine and oak to low chaparral as you climb. Go north on the Riding and Hiking Trail just over a mile to Pine Ridge Trail. The sign here indicates 1½ miles to Green Valley Campground. This trail, following roughly the crest of Pine Ridge, first slashes through a veritable forest of manzanita, then descends along the south facing slopes. An excellent view encompasses the length of Green Valley and the surrounding Sweetwater River drainage from this latter part. At the end of the trail, you arrive at the campground a few hundred yards north of the starting point at Falls Picnic Area.

Green Valley Falls

36

Trip 3, Trail 2 • Airplane Ridge Monument Trail

Approximate distance: 1.5 miles (1 way)
Low point (trailhead): 3,960 feet
High point (Airplane Monument): 4,770 feet

The Monument Trail is a short, easy walk from Green Valley Campground to the monument on Airplane Ridge. The trail begins at the picnic area on the north end of the campground area. After rising through the oak and chaparral slopes overlooking Green Valley, it joins with West Mesa Fire Road. Continue straight ahead and proceed northward about 100 yards, then follow the Monument Trail as it splits off to the left. The appearance of an airplane engine in the middle of the path is an incongruous sight, but a plaque has been set here to explain the details: "In Memory of Col. F. C. Marshall and 1st Lt. C. L. Webber who fell at this spot Dec. 7, 1922." From the monument you may look upon the densely wooded Japacha Creek Canyon below and the cone-shaped profile of Stonewall Peak in the distance.

Airplane Monument

Monument Trail

37

Trip 3, Trail 3 • Dyar Spring Trail

Approximate distance: 5.5 miles round trip
Low point (trailhead): 4,000 feet
High point (East Mesa): 4,760 feet

This loop through terrain typical of the lower elevations and drier portions of the Cuyamaca Mountains includes a stop midway at Dyar Spring, a year-round source of good drinking water. You may conveniently pick up the trail at the Sweetwater River bridge on Highway 79, where parking is allowed during the day. From the parking area take the Harvey Moore Trail, a designated equestrian trail. Two miles ahead Dyar Spring Fire Road, a seldom-used jeep trail, intersects on the left. The open, grassy expanse around you is known as East Mesa. From the intersection you will see an outcropping of white rock on the hillside to the east. Closer inspection (if you are so inclined) will reveal this to be a quartz ledge.

From the Harvey Moore Trail, travel one mile north on Dyar Spring Fire Road to Dyar Spring. There are many small seeps in the area, but if you follow the sign to the left, you'll come to an elevated pipe irregularly gushing with spring-fed water. This is a place not only to fill canteens, but also to cool off one's head and upper body.

Back on the trail again, continue north across tall grass and into the chaparral. The rocky path continues up and over a low ridge, then goes down sharply to the junction of Juaquapin Trail on a wooded saddle. Go left on Juaquapin Trail, following the grassy banks of Juaquapin Creek. Near the junction of the trail that leads south to the Harvey Moore Trail, look under the nearby grove of live oaks and discover several Indian mortar holes. This is one of many such places in the Cuyamaca Mountains where acorns were processed into a nutritious meal.

At the junction stay right (north) and continue to the next junction where the sign reads "Green Valley Camp — 1¾ miles." Follow this trail one mile to the Sweetwater River bridge.

Harper Creek

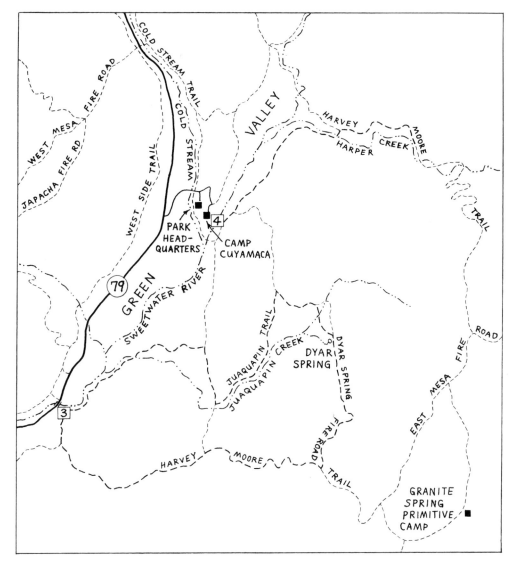

COLD STREAM TRAIL

WEST MESA FIRE ROAD

JAPACHA FIRE RD.

COLD STREAM

WEST SIDE TRAIL

VALLEY

HARVEY

HARPER   CREEK

MOORE

TRAIL

PARK
HEAD-
QUARTERS

4

CAMP
CUYAMACA

79

GREEN

SWEETWATER RIVER

JUAQUAPIN TRAIL

JUAQUAPIN CREEK

DYAR
SPRING

DYAR SPRING

3

HARVEY

MOORE

FIRE ROAD TRAIL

EAST MESA FIRE   ROAD

GRANITE
SPRING
PRIMITIVE
CAMP

Trip 3, Trail 4 ● Harper Creek Trail

Approximate distance: 1.5 miles (1 way)
Low point (Sweetwater River): 4,050 feet
High point: 4,340 feet

The beautiful Harper Creek Canyon, on the east side of Green Valley, is a seldom-visited but unique area of the park. This gorge, cut by a tributary of the Sweetwater River, contains some fascinating examples of water-polished rock. It would be best to avoid this area in the hot summer months since there is little protection from the sun, but it is well suited to exploration during the crisp months of winter and spring.

The quickest and most direct way to reach the canyon is by starting at the park headquarters in Green Valley. You may park free of charge at the Indian exhibit next door. To find the trailhead, walk eastward toward the Sweetwater River. The facilities along the bank of the river — classrooms, playing fields, and a swimming pool — are part of Camp Cuyamaca, a San Diego city and county school camp.

A path leads from the baseball diamond near the swimming pool to a log bridge across the Sweetwater River. Some water, at least, will be found here at any time of the year. Take the path leading north along the east side of the river and across Green Valley. When you arrive at the mouth of Harper Creek Canyon, walk upstream following the creek bed. Water flows here during the winter and spring, but dries up into isolated pools or disappears altogether during the summer. You may do some rock scrambling, so be careful on wet days when the smooth rock at the bottom of the canyon becomes very slippery.

About a half-mile up, the rock disappears and the canyon becomes overgrown with vegetation. To your left you'll see the Harvey Moore Equestrian trail, and you may follow this back to the mouth of the canyon. The trail climbs about 100 feet above the creek before dropping down again. You then return via the same route to Camp Cuyamaca.

Log bridge over Sweetwater River

40

View east from Stonewall Peak

Trip 3, Trail 5 • Stonewall Peak Trail

Approximate distance: 2.0 miles to Stonewall Peak, 5.5 miles for loop through Los Caballos Camp
Elevation at trailhead: 4,870 feet
High point (Stonewall Peak): 5,730 feet
Low point (Los Caballos Camp): 4,720 feet

The most popular trail of the Cuyamaca area is the one from Paso Picacho Campground to the top of Stonewall Peak. This switchback route up the west side of the mountain gains nearly 1,000 feet in two miles; but is not difficult, even for the novice hiker. Just beyond the dense stand of incense cedar midway up the trail, the panorama begins to unfold. As you climb higher you may see Cuyamaca Reservoir to the north. Beyond the lake is a large meadow — actually the dry bed of the reservoir. During years of normal rainfall the lake is confined to the small area in the foreground, and the remaining area provides forage for livestock.

Vegetation thins out near the top, and in the final hundred feet a guardrail and steps cut into the granite are provided. The scene encompasses the entire Cuyamaca and Laguna Mountain region, although distant views are cut off by foreground ranges in the east and west. This is a good place to identify and photograph the major peaks of the main Cuyamaca range: from north to south they are North Peak, Middle Peak, Cuyamaca Peak, and Japacha Peak. Highway 79 is the grey ribbon running from Cuyamaca Reservoir on the north, across the saddle connecting Stonewall and Cuyamaca Peaks, through Green Valley to the southern end of the park.

If you want to return to Paso Picacho Campground by a longer route, retrace your steps a few hundred feet down the Stonewall Peak Trail. From here a trail branches northward through a broken gate. Steep and rocky at first, it levels off later, passing near Little Stonewall Peak then dropping gradually toward the California Riding and Hiking Trail near Los Caballos Horsemen's Camp. You will travel a one-mile segment of this trail, which is part of what was once designed to be a continuous series of trails and dirt roads running the length of California. Many sections were never built or pieced together, and some sections in San Diego County have been abandoned because of easement difficulties. Fortunately, the nearly completed Pacific Crest Trail (see Trip 4) serves as a good replacement.

Remain on the east side of Highway 79 when the Riding and Hiking Trail forks to the west. Paso Picacho Campground is then a half-mile down the trail paralleling the road.

Stonewall Peak Trail

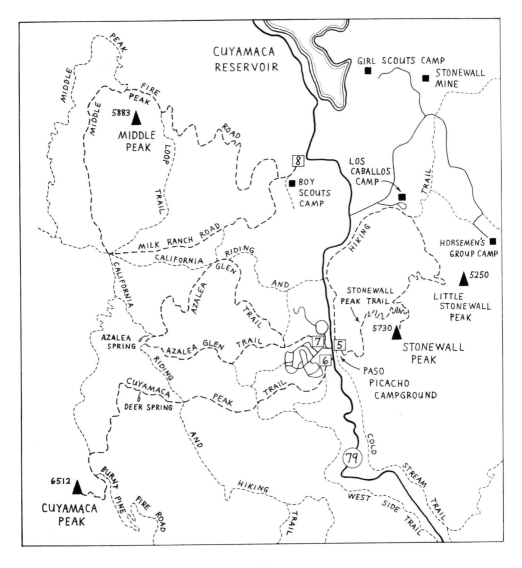

Trip 3, Trail 6 ● Cuyamaca Peak Trail

Approximate distance: 3.5 miles (1 way)
Low point (trailhead): 4,870 feet
High point (Cuyamaca Peak): 6,512 feet

Here is a most interesting trail (actually a smooth paved road) to the highest peak in the Cuyamaca Mountains. This one-lane truck trail, closed to public vehicles, begins at the 4,870-foot elevation of the Forest Service fire station adjacent to Paso Picacho Campground, and winds steadily uphill to the 6,512-foot summit of Cuyamaca Peak. In addition to some eyecatching scenery, a spring along the way provides you with welcome refreshment.

You may pick up the road at its intersection with Highway 79 just south of the entrance to the campground. The going is easy at first as the trail skirts the edge of the camping area. Look behind you to see the rocky summit of Stonewall Peak standing tall through the trees.

After crossing the California Riding and Hiking Trail just over a mile from the campground, the trail steepens considerably. The trees thin out, being replaced by chaparral. The luxury of shade is now left behind, but the sound of running water soon heralds your arrival at Deer Spring.

Observing the many forms of wildlife attracted to the spring is a good excuse to linger here for a while. The hummingbird is perhaps the most fascinating to watch, as it hovers briefly over the stream for a sip. Look out for that bumble bee, though! In summer the flying insects swarming around this spot of moisture may provide an incentive to move on somewhat prematurely.

With fresh water in hand, you may now tackle the unrelenting upslope before you. Soon you come upon the weird, distorted shapes of long-dead pine trees — the unfortunate victims of an extremely hot forest fire which exploded across the park in 1950. These snags, however, do offer excellent photographic possibilities, particularly with the surrounding mountains and desert as a backdrop.

An appropriately named Burnt Pine Fire Road forks off to the left. Then, with a final burst of energy, you will reach the antenna-bewhiskered summit. It's easy to see why a fire lookout tower was, until recently, located here. The view is incomparable. Palomar Observatory's 200-inch telescope dome may be glimpsed as a tiny silvery speck of light on the dark ridge 30 miles to the north. San Diego and the Pacific Ocean are seen to the west, haze permitting; in the south, a succession of ever-distant ridges marches deep into Baja California. The desert view in the east is somewhat blocked by the Laguna Mountains, although on clear days the Salton Sea may be seen to the northeast.

Far below you is the starting point at Paso Picacho Campground, and beyond this is our old friend, Stonewall Peak, which has now shrunk to a mere dimple on the landscape. Returning to Paso Picacho, you may watch Stonewall loom larger against the sky attaining its former glory as you descend.

Southeast of Cuyamaca Peak the rare Cuyamaca cypress has established a foothold within its sole habitat on the steep slopes of the headwaters of King Creek. So limited is its restricted range that the area is known as a tree island. The Cuyamaca cypress is currently experiencing a recovery, after it was all but wiped out in the fire of 1950.

When you return — instead of taking the paved road all the way back — you might wish to detour north on the California Riding and Hiking Trail to pick up Azalea Glen Trail for the remainder of the hike.

Pine snag below Cuyamaca Peak

Trip 3, Trail 7 • Azalea Glen Trail

Approximate distance: 3.0 miles round trip
Elevation at trailhead: 4,850 feet
Low point: 4,800 feet
High point (Azalea Spring): 5,370 feet

Hiking the Azalea Glen Trail is ideal for those who wish to enjoy an hour or two of the best Cuyamaca scenery — indeed, some of the finest scenery Southern California has to offer. Special attractions are found in every season along this trail: wildflowers running riot over the meadows in the spring, plentiful shade in the summertime, crisp weather and autumn color in the fall, and a snow-dusted landscape in winter.

The well-marked trail begins at Paso Picacho Campground just across the parking lot from the picnic area. Later it divides into two forks. If you take the right fork here, you follow the loop counterclockwise. For the most part the path travels through the mixed pine, fir, cedar, and oak forest which is typical of this area, but occasionally you'll run into open meadows. Watch for the Indian mortar holes on the flat granite rocks along the trail when you enter the first large clearing after the fork.

Azalea Glen Trail briefly joins the California Riding and Hiking Trail about one mile from the campground. For a short distance here the trail is accompanied by a small arroyo, which in periods of rain or snowfall becomes a sparkling brook. The trail then heads sharply uphill to Azalea Spring, another of those delightful refreshment spots common in this area. The remainder of this walk takes you directly back to Paso Picacho Campground.

Azalea Glen Trail

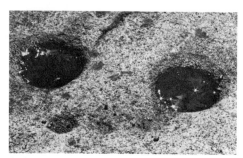

Indian Mortar Holes

Trip 3, Trail 8 • Middle Peak Loop Trail

Approximate distance: 5.5 miles round trip
Low point (trailhead): 4,660 feet
High point: 5,710 feet

Little else distinguishes Middle Peak from neighboring mountains in the main Cuyamaca range other than its exceptionally well-forested upper slopes. Unlike the Cuyamaca and North Peak summits, Middle Peak has not suffered seriously in recent times from the effects of forest fires. Lovers of the deep, dark forest will undoubtedly appreciate the type of environment found here. There are few places in Southern California such as this where one can actually lose the sense of direction in broad daylight.

Middle Peak is a low-profile, roughly cone-shaped mountain overlooking Cuyamaca Reservoir to the east. The loop described here begins on Highway 79 at the north end of the park (near the reservoir) and encircles Middle Peak on fire roads. You may park (well off the road) near the entrance to the Boy Scouts Camp Hual-Cu-Cuish. From Highway 79, take this entrance road (Milk Ranch Road) a few hundred yards to the southwest. The sign at the intersection of Milk Ranch Road and Middle Peak Fire Road indicates a distance of two miles to Middle Peak Loop Trail. Follow Middle Peak Fire Road as it zigzags upward. As you climb the scenery changes from black oak trees to incense cedar, to giant ponderosa and sugar pines. When you reach Middle Peak Loop Trail, take the right hand branch. No trail leads to the top of the peak from here, even though the summit is only a short distance away. Furthermore, distant views are not available from the top as they are blocked by dense vegetation on all sides.

Follow Middle Peak Loop Trail as it contours around the north side of the mountain, and remain on the loop trail after you reach the second junction with Middle Peak Fire Road. In the next mile you'll descend along the west and south facing slopes to the six-way intersection at the base of the mountain. The trees thin out near the bottom, allowing a good view of the dry foothills to the west and the Pacific Ocean on the distant horizon. At the intersection you may pick up Milk Ranch Road, which will return you to the starting point.

Milk Ranch Road Overlook

47

area map – Julian, Cuyamaca Mountains, Laguna Mountains

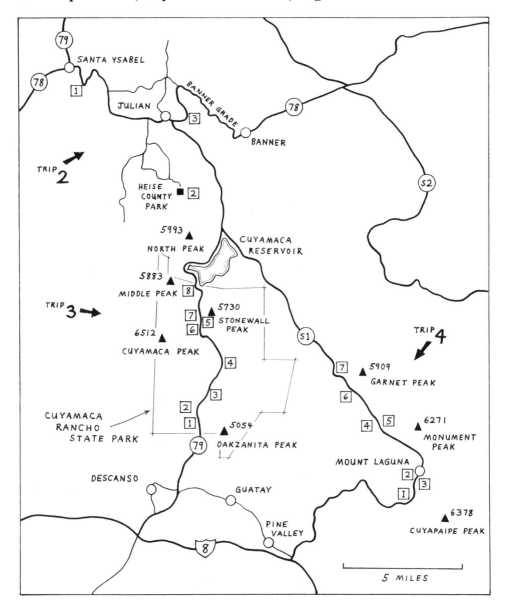

Ponderosa Pine Bark

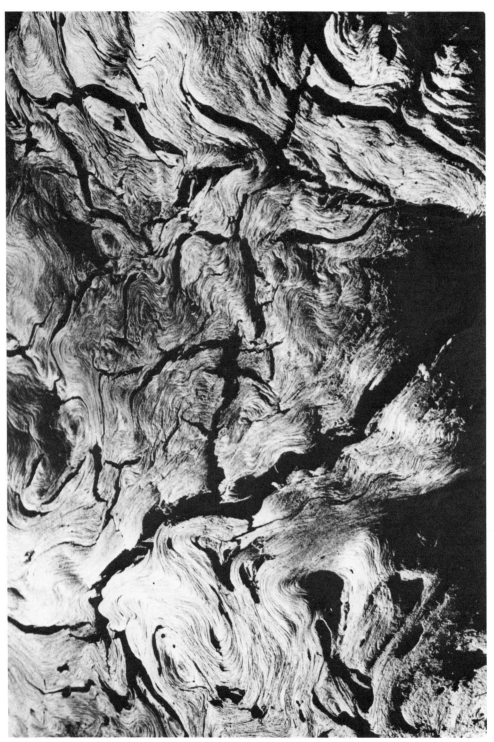

Nature's Artistry

Trip 4 • The Laguna Mountains

Campgrounds: Laguna Campground, Burnt Rancheria Campground, Cibbets Flat Campground

Picnic Grounds: Desert View Picnic Ground, Pioneer Mail Picnic Ground

Desert-bordering mountain ranges are not uncommon in Southern California, but their surprising contrasts inspire wonder in the thousands of visitors who explore them each year. Of these ranges, the Laguna Mountains are the most easily accessible to San Diegans. The pine-crested slopes of these mountains wring out most of the remaining precipitation from moisture-laden coastal clouds moving inland from the Pacific ocean. Only a meager amount is spared for the Colorado Desert which lies in the rain shadow to the east. The Anza-Borrego Desert State Park, at the foot of the Lagunas, occupies nearly a thousand square miles of this rugged desert.

The majority of the land in the Laguna Mountains is administered by the Cleveland National Forest, although many pockets of privately owned property are also represented here. The Forest Service has developed elaborate facilities in the Laguna Mountain Recreation Area to accommodate the large number of visitors. In addition to camping and picnicking, evening campfire lecture programs, conducted by a ranger-naturalist, highlight weekend evenings during the summer.

The Laguna Mountains are considered an excellent dark-sky observing site for astronomical research, a distinction shared with the Palomar Mountains. For this reason, San Diego State University has located its observatory here. A visitor program at the observatory is operated in conjunction with the Forest Service on weekend evenings from June to August.

Several trails in the Laguna Mountain Recreation Area permit detailed exploration of the region. Four of these are popular self-guided nature trails. Most provide good views of the surrounding mountains and their relationship to the desert.

From San Diego you may reach the La-guna Mountains in just a little more than an hour. The drive is, moreover, a good opportunity to observe a wide cross-section of the terrain and vegetation of San Diego County. Take Interstate 8 east through the El Cajon Valley and the brushy foothill country of Alpine and Descanso. The low scrub gives way to a few scattered oaks and pines at the nearly 4000-foot elevation of Pine Valley. Sunrise Highway (County S1), intersecting from the left, is your gateway to the lofty summits ahead.

The highway first snakes along dry Scove Canyon, but after a few miles, you are aware of a startling transition: the landscape is now dominated by a mixed forest of oak and pine, while the temperature drops perceptibly. Soon the scene is predominantly Jeffrey pine forest, and before long you pass scattered cabins and Burnt Rancheria Campground, then arrive at the village of Mount Laguna. The town, with architecture resembling that of High Sierra resorts, offers the conveniences of a motel, summer cabins, market and restaurants. A Forest Service information office is also located here.

Continuing on, the Desert View Picnic Area is on your right just beyond the 6,000-foot elevation sign. The view is spectacular, but is equalled or excelled from points further down the road.

Now the road turns northwest. On the right a spur road leads 1/4 mile to Vista Point on the slopes of Stephenson Peak. On top of the peak are the domes of a decommissioned Air Force radar station. Straight ahead on Sunrise Highway are Laguna Campground and Pioneer Mail Picnic Ground, three and six miles, respectively, from Mount Laguna.

For a slightly longer, but scenic return to San Diego, continue driving northwest on Sunrise Highway past Pioneer Mail Picnic Ground. Several good views of the desert may be had from the road, but pull off on the spur road to Kwaaymii Point for an even more inclusive view. Arriving at Highway 79 near Cuyamaca Reservoir, you may either turn south through the Cuyamaca Mountains and rejoin Interstate 8 near Descanso, or you may turn north toward Julian. From Julian, Highway 78 leads west toward the coast.

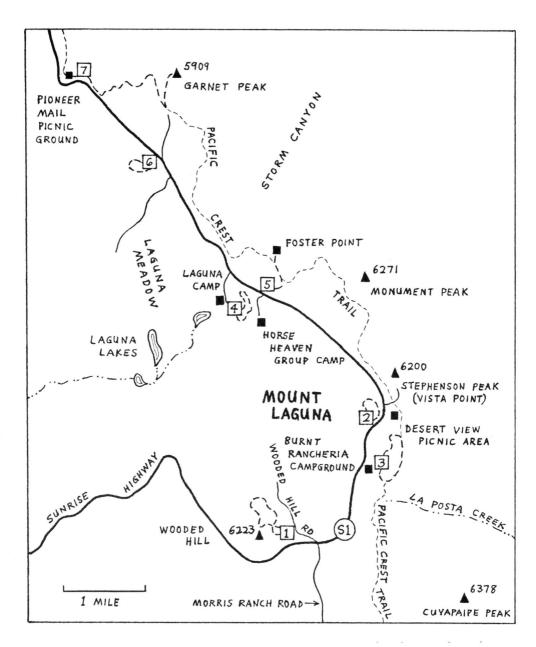

5909
GARNET PEAK

PIONEER
MAIL
PICNIC
GROUND

PACIFIC

CREST

STORM CANYON

FOSTER POINT

6271
MONUMENT PEAK

LAGUNA
MEADOW

LAGUNA
CAMP

TRAIL

HORSE
HEAVEN
GROUP CAMP

LAGUNA
LAKES

6200
STEPHENSON PEAK
(VISTA POINT)

MOUNT
LAGUNA

DESERT VIEW
PICNIC AREA

BURNT
RANCHERIA
CAMPGROUND

WOODED HILL RD

SUNRISE HIGHWAY

WOODED
HILL

6223

LA POSTA CREEK

PACIFIC CREST TRAIL

1 MILE

MORRIS RANCH ROAD →

6378
CUYAPAIPE PEAK

Trip 4, Trail 1 • Wooded Hill Loop Trail

Approximate distance: 1.5 miles round trip
Low point (trailhead): 5,960 feet
High point (Wooded Hill): 6,223 feet

The Wooded Hill Trail is one of four self-guided nature trails in the Laguna Mountain Recreation Area. It's a good trail to start with if you wish to become familiar with the native flora and fauna.

The trailhead is on Wooded Hill Road, which intersects Sunrise Highway about two miles southwest of the town of Mount Laguna. A box containing trail guides will be found at the small parking area which marks the beginning of the trail.

Jeffrey pine, black oak, incense cedar, and several varieties of common chaparral plants are highlighted in the trail guide. In addition to learning about the vegetation, this is a good area to listen for and observe wildlife. Gray squirrels flit about the branches and underbrush, while acorn woodpeckers are busy chipping holes into the trunks of pine trees to make holes for acorn storage.

The trail winds through a well-forested area to the top of Wooded Hill (elevation 6,223 feet), where a plexiglass covered map indicates the location of the major peaks visible along the horizon. On exceptionally clear days San Diego and the Pacific Ocean offer an unmatched panorama. Look for Point Loma — the southward pointing peninsula that serves as breakwater for the northern portion of San Diego Bay. Nearby, the silvery domes seen on the ridge to the southeast are part of the Mount Laguna Observatory.

Trip 4, Trail 2 • Kwaaymii Trail

Approximate distance: 0.5 mile round trip
Low point (trailhead): 5,920 feet
High point: 6,020 feet

This very short walk begins at the Cleveland National Forest Visitor Information Office in Mount Laguna, encircles a small hill behind the town, then returns to the information office.

Up until the present century, the Laguna Mountains were summer home to bands of Kumeyaay Indians, specifically a sub-tribe known as the Kwaaymii. Plaques set along this trail explain the Indians' use of native shrubs and trees for food, shelter, clothing, medicinal and ceremonial uses. The Indians were able to live adequately on the natural yield of many different types of vegetation, while supplementing their diet with small game. It is interesting to note that these early natives not only were familiar with the basic concepts of ecology, but also put into practice conservation of natural resources in their everyday lives. As an example, while gathering acorns, the squaws would leave a certain number behind to insure future generation of oak trees.

A site at the top of the hill was used for processing of acorns. Bedrock mortars (deep holes) and metates (shallow depressions) may be seen along the trail. Acorns were pounded into meal in these grinding holes as the first step in the production of edible food such as soup, pudding, or bread.

Plaque on Wooded Hill

Trip 4, Trail 3 • Desert View Nature Trail

Approximate distance: 1.2 miles round trip
Low point (trailhead): 5,930 feet
High point: 6,050 feet

A large parking area has been set aside in Burnt Rancheria Campground for users of the Desert View Nature Trail. Trail guide booklets are available at the beginning detailing the points of interest along the way. Due to the popularity of this walk, many false trails cut by people wandering off the path may present a bit of difficulty, but small cactus-shaped markers or numbered posts help guide the way at critical points.

The highlights are two vistas — the first overlooks Cuyapaipe Indian Reservation land along La Posta Creek, and the second provides a panoramic view of the Colorado Desert. Both spots afford excellent opportunities for photography, especially with a wide angle lens, to encompass a large part of the view or a telephoto lens to simulate aerial photos of the desert floor below.

Tree Killed by Dwarf Mistletoe

Trip 4, Trail 4 • Lightning Ridge Trail

Approximate distance: 1.2 miles round trip
Low point (trailhead): 5,570 feet
High point (Lightning Ridge): 5,800 feet

The amphitheater at Laguna Campground is the starting point for the Lightning Ridge Trail. This is a popular loop trail and again the problem of false paths may be encountered. Go 100 yards southeast from the trailhead (marked by a sign), then take the trail on the left which intersects sharply and heads uphill. From the top of the ridge you may look down upon Laguna Meadow and Little Laguna Lake, one of the lakes that lend their name to the Laguna Mountains. ("Laguna" is the Spanish word for "lake".) The existence of these lakes is highly ephemeral — Little Laguna Lake is usually seen as a dry lake bed.

Chula Vista Reservoir, on the trail summit, is part of the water supply serving camping areas at the bottom of the hill. From here Lightning Ridge Trail descends along the other side of the ridge, crosses a dirt road, then finally returns to the amphitheater.

Dandelions along Lightning Ridge Trail

Trip 4, Trail 5 • Foster Point

Approximate distance: 0.5 mile (1 way)
Low point (trailhead): 5,640 feet
High point (Foster Point): 5,740 feet

A good view of the Colorado Desert through Storm Canyon is the main attraction of this brief off-road excursion. Drive two miles northwest of Mount Laguna to the entrance to Horse Heaven Group Campground. Park on either side of the road.

Begin walking east up a faint former road/trail through the Jeffrey pine forest. This was once part of the Laguna Rim Trail, which now has been incorporated into the Pacific Crest Trail. After about 1/3 mile, in an area called Flathead Flats, the faint path turns north and approaches a well-defined narrow footpath — the Pacific Crest Trail. Follow this to the point at which the trail runs out of the pine forest and into dense chaparral. Walk about 200 feet farther, then take the small trail intersecting on the right. This trail winds about 300 feet through the brush, and ends at Foster Point. A metal plaque placed by the Sierra Club indicates the directions and distances of the many landmarks visible from the point. Included is Southern California's highest mountain, San Gorgonio, in the San Bernadino Mountains. Clear, crisp winter days are required for viewing the distant peaks, but even on a hazy day the desert dropoff is spectacular, and the photographic possibilities nearly unlimited.

Foster Point

56

Trip 4, Trail 6 ● Witches' Broom Trail

Approximate distance: 0.5 mile round trip
Trail elevation: 5,350 feet

You may already have noticed the effects wrought by a crippling parasite upon the Jeffrey pines of the Laguna Mountains. Dwarf mistletoe is responsible for the enlarged limbs and the prolific branching known as "witches' brooms" that afflict many of the older trees.

The Witches' Broom self-guided nature trail explains the nature of the dwarf mistletoe problem and the efforts of the Forest Service to control it. Along the trail you will see the world's largest witches' broom, supported by a 4-foot diameter lower limb on a Jeffrey pine that is more than 300 years old.

World's largest Witches' Broom

Trip 4, Trail 7 ● Garnet Peak

Approximate distance: 2.3 miles (1 way)
Low point (trailhead): 5,250 feet
High point (Garnet Peak): 5,909 feet

Of the many desert view points afforded by road or trail in the Laguna Mountains, my favorite is Garnet Peak. The most interesting route to the top originates at Pioneer Mail Picnic Ground, and utilizes a portion of the Pacific Crest Trail. Pioneer Mail Picnic Ground is located on Sunrise Highway about six miles northwest of the town of Mount Laguna.

While driving toward the picnic ground from Mount Laguna, you can glimpse the desert to the east. Garnet Peak may be seen from here, too, looking more like the edge of a precipice than a peak. A marker at the pine and oak shaded picnic area commemorates the "jackass mail" — the first transcontinental mail route from Texas to San Diego named for the pack animals used to haul the mail across the mountains.

The dirt parking lot in front of the picnic tables also serves as the trailhead. Follow the Pacific Crest Trail southeast, paralleling the Sunrise Highway. Soon the trail turns away from the road, breaks out of the trees, then contours along the chaparral-covered slopes. An occasional black oak may be seen here out in the open. These are the survivors of the destructive fires which have swept through in past years.

The unmarked trail to Garnet peak intersects the Pacific Crest Trail about two miles from the picnic ground. Here is a rocky but not excessively steep climb. Near the top the chaparral cover is predominantly manzanita.

The view from the pile of rocks at the top is nothing less than stupendous, so be sure to carry your camera with you. On three sides the peak falls away sharply to the desert floor. Look for the blue arc of the Salton Sea to the northeast. One word of caution here: on windy days make certain you have a good foothold on the rocks!

Manzanita and Yucca-Garnet Peak

Cholla Cactus – Anza-Borrego Desert

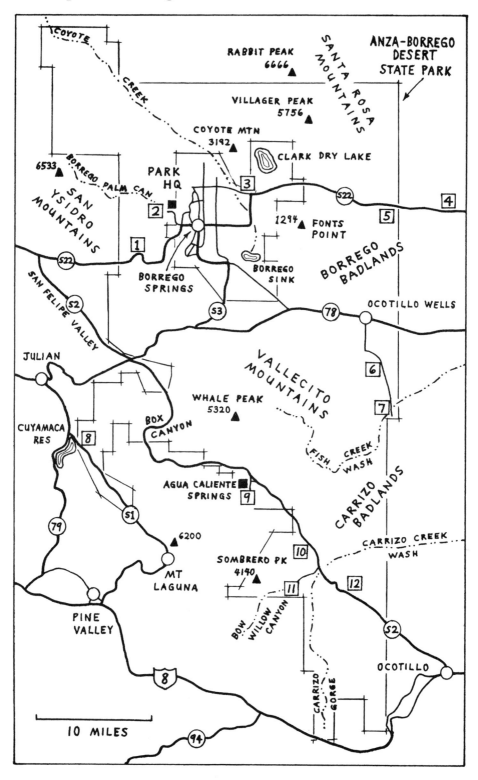

Smoke Tree

THE DESERT EXPERIENCE

California is a land of contrasts, and San Diego County is a microcosm of the state's diversity. The eastern part of the county, in particular, represents the hot, dry end of the geographical spectrum. Here, along the eastern edge of the coastal mountains and extending into Arizona, is the Colorado Desert, some of the lowest, hottest and loneliest real estate in America. The impression of many persons on seeing this desert for the first time is distinctly negative. It appears stark and somehow alien — not consistent with their concept of a green planet earth. But given the chance, the desert will reveal its mysteries and charms to those who are open-minded enough to explore it.

Try spending a day hiking in the desert. When your automobile is left behind, and the sound of traffic along the highway fades away, you will find yourself alone and deeply involved with the elemental forces of nature around you. Senses become sharpened to an extraordinary degree, allowing insights never before experienced. The alien quality of the desert seems reinforced: the sun appears somehow larger than life, pouring radiation upon the shimmering landscape; the air, devoid of moisture, catches in the throat; brittle, thorny plants cling steadfastly to life, rooted in rock or sand; the diminutive sound of a scurrying animal or alarmed bird cracks the all-pervading silence. All of these impressions contribute to the breadth of the desert experience. But this is not all.

Slowly, but inevitably, comes the realization that the desert isn't really alien and inhospitable. It appears to be lifeless at first glance, yet careful observation reveals evidence of many forms of plant and animal life, active or dormant. The wildflower bloom after spring rains is proof of the regenerative abilities of desert vegetation, and the coming of nightfall brings forth multitudes of nocturnal animals.

In spite of its sometimes threatening appearance, the desert can be quite hospitable to human beings. Actually, it is the California desert itself that needs protection from man. Motorcycles and off-road vehicles do have legitimate uses on approved routes of travel, but too often the indiscriminate use of these machines by ignorant adventurers upsets the delicate ecological balance and mars the beauty of the desert. Travel by foot, on the other hand, runs a negligible

Young Barrel Cactus

risk of disturbing the fragile environment, and lets you experience most effectively the unique sights, sounds and smells of the desert. Only by acquiring sensitivity to the desert environment may you come to know the desert, and consequently love it.

When traveling in the desert, take plenty of extra water along in the car. Bring a shovel if you intend to turn off the paved roads. Don't underestimate your capacity for drinking water on the trail — it's always safer to bring more than you need. Finally, you may enjoy your desert experience much more by hiking in the early morning or late afternoon, especially on hot days. At times like these, shadows provide welcome relief and the subdued colors of the desert landscape are enhanced by the low sun angle.

Borrego Badlands from Font's Point

Trip 5 ● The Anza-Borrego Desert

Points of Interest: Too numerous to mention

Campgrounds: Borrego Palm Canyon Campground, Tamarisk Grove Campground, and Bow Willow Campground in Anza-Borrego Desert State Park; also campgrounds at Old Vallecito Stage Station County Park and Agua Caliente Springs County Park

Primitive Campgrounds: Sheep Canyon, Fish Creek, Little Pass, Yaqui Pass, Yaqui Well, Arroyo Salado, Mountain Palm Springs, Culp Valley, and Dos Cabezas in Anza-Borrego Desert State Park.

Picnic Grounds: at the main campgrounds

The Anza-Borrego Desert is truly one of the more extraordinary deserts of the United States. In it you will find nearly every interesting aspect associated with the Colorado Desert of California — that vast expanse of arid land stretching across the foot of California from the Colorado River to the slopes of the Peninsular Range.

Most of the western portion of the Colorado Desert, from the mountains to the Salton Sea basin, has the distinction of being included in a desert state park, the boundaries of which are flung far and wide. The Anza-Borrego Desert State Park is the largest state park in the United States, encompassing nearly a thousand square miles within extreme limits 60 miles long and 30 miles wide. The "low" desert of the Salton Sink with its characteristic badlands and alkali flats is found here, as well as the palm canyons and serene pinyon pine and juniper mountains of the "high" desert. A good network of paved roads, and a much more extensive system of dirt roads suitable for off-road vehicles penetrates the interior of the park, also allowing many opportunities for exploration on foot. I've included 12 trails in this section, an adequate number for the purposes of this book, but a far from complete list of places to see. The backpacker will find almost unlimited prospects. Park literature declines to list all the major points of interest in the park, with the explanation that they haven't all been discovered yet!

Borrego Palm Canyon

64

Pinyon Snag — Santa Rosa Mountains

An introduction to the Anza-Borrego Desert would not be complete without a few brief comments on its history. The area has known a succession of human inhabitants in the last few thousand years, as evidenced by shelters and artifacts left behind. Since the drying up of the ancient fresh-water Lake Cahuilla, which occupied the present-day Salton Sink, Kumeyaay and Cahuilla Indians had populated oases and canyons fed by water that was more plentiful than today. The Indians were nomadic, traveling in small bands, and occupying various camping sites according to the season. Fruit, foliage and fiber from low desert plants and the pinyon and oak of higher elevations provided the raw materials for survival in a harsh environment. Small-game hunting and trading with other tribes rounded out their lifestyle. Archeologically significant Indian sites are common in the Anza-Borrego today, and it is likely that many others have not yet been discovered.

The late eighteenth century saw the first attempts to establish a land route connecting the Spanish settlements and missions at Sonora, Mexico, to the coast of California. Juan Bautista de Anza was the first Spaniard to do so. His passage included a trek across Borrego Valley and Coyote Canyon, two well-known areas of the park. Earlier, Pedro Fages had descended into the Anza-Borrego area from the mountains to the west, thus claiming credit for the first journey by white men into the California desert. Incidentally, the "Borrego" part of the name Anza-Borrego comes from the Spanish word for big horn sheep, some of which occasionally can be seen in remote areas.

Eventually, an emigrant trail through Carrizo Corridor (the series of valleys roughly paralleling County Highway S2 in the southern part of the park) and San Felipe Valley bore the traffic of gold-seeking California pioneers. The turn of the century saw limited grazing and agriculture in the valleys. Finally, in 1928, state park authorities, seeking to preserve a desert expanse, chose this area because of its outstanding natural features and valuable heritage. An aggressive acquisition program has continued to the present day, with the result being a 620,000-acre Anza-Borrego Desert State Park.

A first examination of the Anza-Borrego Desert should probably begin with a visit to Borrego Springs and park headquarters at Borrego Palm Canyon. Due to a rather unusual arrangement — a result of the acquisition program — the town of Borrego Springs, and most of Borrego Valley that surrounds it, is not included in the park. It is a political island of privately owned land within the park, completely surrounded by the park. You will find that the small business district around Christmas Circle in the middle of town has all the conveniences of a first-class resort.

Two main entrances serve Borrego Springs and the northern half of the park. You may take Highway 78 east from Julian, descend the Banner Grade to Earthquake Valley and enter the west boundary of the park at Sentenac Canyon, then turn north on County Highway S3 over Yaqui Pass to Borrego Valley. Or you may drive north from Santa Ysabel on Highway 79, past Lake Henshaw to S2, then continue eastward on S22 down the Montezuma Grade to Borrego Valley. The north half of the park is the most popular, and includes the favorite points of interest. Borrego Palm Canyon and the tributaries of Coyote Canyon are the best examples of the steep mountain and palm canyon territory west of Borrego Valley. On the other side of the valley is the Borrego Badlands, an example of the most barren and forbidding kind of desert in California. The four-mile dirt road from Borrego-Salton Seaway to Font's Point may not be suitable for passenger cars (4-wheel-drive OK), but it affords the best view of the badlands from above.

The southern half of the park, on the other hand, is largely neglected, but for no good reason. County Highway S2, running from Highway 78 in the middle of the park to Interstate 8 at the southern end, allows ready access to the mountains and valleys along the west side. The major state park campground of the south half, Bow Willow Campground, is located along this road as are two county parks, Old Vallecito Stage Station and Agua Caliente Springs. The Carrizo Badlands to the east is perhaps the most fascinating area. Not only does it include outstanding geological features, but it also contains fossil beds providing, as one scientist says, "one of the most remarkably complete sequences of animal life to be found anywhere in the world."

The Anza-Borrego Desert, then, may be thought of as the last frontier of San Diego County. Nowhere else will you find the untamed qualities peculiar to the wide-open spaces beyond the mountains — the peace, the silence, the freedom of spirit. We must be thankful that it belongs to all of us.

Borrego Valley from Mining Prospect in Santa Rosa Mountains

Trip 5, Trail 1 • Culp Valley Outlook

Approximate Distance: 0.5 mile (1 way)
Low point (trailhead): 3,340 feet
High point (Vista Point): 3,520 feet

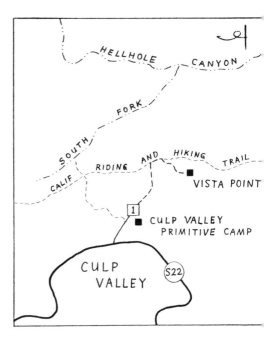

Of the three paved roads leading into the Anza-Borrego Desert State Park from the west, the Montezuma-Borrego Highway (County S22) makes the most spectacular approach. From Ranchita, at the edge of the Montezuma Valley plateau, the road literally carves itself through rock in the ten-mile descent to Borrego Valley. Numerous turnouts are provided along the road for those who like to gape at the scenery. If you wish to enjoy a view of the desert floor without the noise and distraction of passing traffic, however, there is another lookout point located some distance off the road and accessible by a trail originating at Culp Valley primitive camp.

The primitive camp is located north of the highway approximately three miles east of the park boundary. You may park here and walk northward on the dirt road leading up to the ridge dividing Culp Valley from the Hellhole Canyon drainage. A branch of the California Riding and Hiking Trail (which at this point roughly parallels Highway S22 to Borrego Valley) is briefly joined here. Follow the sign to "Vista Point," 400 yards beyond.

San Ysidro Mountain, capped by a series of cone-like peaks (the largest of which is known as The Thimble), rears up to the north and west, while Borrego Valley shimmers below at the mouth of appropriately named Hellhole Canyon. You are standing nearly 3,000 feet above the valley floor at this point, and the photographic possibilities are magnificent.

Split Rock at Culp Valley Vista Point

68

Borrego Valley and Santa Rosa Mountains from Culp Valley Vista Point

Trip 5, Trail 2 ● Borrego Palm Canyon

Approximate distance: 1.5 miles (1 way)
Low point (trailhead): 840 feet
High point (palm oasis): 1,250 feet

Hiking the Borrego Palm Canyon nature trail is a desirable prerequisite to further exploration of the Anza-Borrego. Here you will find some of the more appreciated aspects of the desert, and perhaps learn to recognize many of the common features characteristic of the area. The highlight is, of course, the large grove of native *Washingtonia filifera* fan palm trees at the end of the trail – a popular place for photographers.

Palm canyons are not unique to the Anza-Borrego Desert. Native palms are, in fact, scattered throughout the Colorado Desert – especially in the well-watered canyons of the east-facing slopes of the highest mountain ranges. In terms of sheer numbers, Borrego Palm Canyon cannot boast of the thousands of palms that line the canyons south of Palm Springs or the little-known furrows of the Sierra San Pedro Martir in Baja California. But probably you will not find a better display that is both easily accessible and under public ownership. As you might expect, the trail to the palms carries a steady stream of visitors during the first few months of the year; in the heat of summer, you will find peaceful solitude here – and a desert oasis all to yourself.

The trailhead is in the west corner of the sprawling Borrego Palm Canyon Campground, north of the new Anza-Borrego Visitor Center, and northwest of Borrego Springs. A small fee will cover picnicking or hiking for the day. Be sure to pick up the informative leaflet for the trail, as it describes many of the common types of cacti, shrubs and trees indigenous to this and other canyons of the Colorado Desert. Descriptions of wildlife and geological formations are included also.

In the first mile the trail winds gradually upward across the alluvium at the mouth of the canyon. You will catch a glimpse of the first group of palms just before entering the V-shaped gorge. The first sight of these clustered palms on a bright, sunny day is quite startling. Contrasted with the rock of the canyon walls, the bright green foliage seems to give off its own radiant light.

Moisture supporting this palm oasis is present year-round, but unless you arrive shortly after a good rain, you may find only isolated seeps and shallow pools. In dry periods most of the water flows underground.

The established trail comes to an end at the first and largest of the palm groves, but you may continue up the canyon through the brush and boulders to the other groves. In addition, an alternate trail returns to the campground. This trail, which branches off the main trail at the mouth of the canyon, adds about 300 yards, but allows a good look at the large numbers of ocotillo that thrive on the upper portion of the alluvial fan.

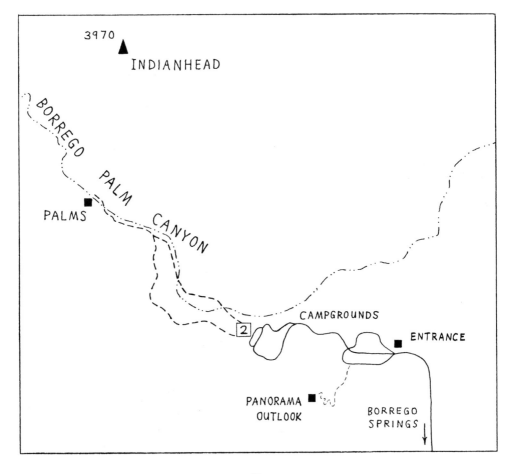

3970
INDIANHEAD

BORREGO PALM CANYON

PALMS

CAMPGROUNDS

2

ENTRANCE

PANORAMA
OUTLOOK

BORREGO
SPRINGS

Trip 5, Trail 3 • Coyote Mountain

Approximate distance: 3.0 miles (1 way)
Low point (trailhead): 620 feet
High point: 1,620 feet

Coyote Mountain stands at the northeast corner of Borrego Valley. As seen from the valley, it presents a surface no less brown and wrinkled than elephant hide. In spite of its lack of inherent attractiveness, it does offer some excellent vantage points to view and photograph that geographical and political island in the desert known as Borrego Springs.

The jeep trail up the south end of Coyote Mountain, itself a part of the state park, offers an easy approach to the barren slopes overlooking the valley. To reach the base of the mountain from Borrego Springs, follow County Highway S22 east along Palm Canyon Drive and north along Pegleg Road to the Pegleg Smith Monument. Here you will find a large pile of rocks, the monument commemorating a famous desert loner and the legend of his lost gold. Adding ten stones, so the story goes, will bring you good luck; removing any will have exactly the opposite effect.

Pick up the jeep trail by walking eastward along the base of the mountain. Once over the top of the first ridge you enter a different world, where vivid blue skies above contrast with the muted colors of the raw soil and rock beneath your feet. Only the distant buzz of motorcycles and dune-buggies on the valley floor disturbs the tranquillity of this place on weekends. Clark Valley to the east is backed up by the heavily eroded Santa Rosa Mountains, and the Borrego-Salton Seaway skims across the sand toward Coachella Valley and the Salton Sink.

Climbing higher you begin to take in the entire Borrego Valley. Nestled against San Ysidro Mountain in the west is the town of Borrego Springs and its largely unfilled subdivision plots. De Anza Desert Country Club makes a green splotch at the mouth of Henderson Canyon, and the tamarisk-lined fields form a checkerboard across the far side of the valley.

Approximately three miles from the monument, the jeep trail begins to fade out. You have now climbed a thousand feet above the valley floor. A less well-defined jeep trail on the next ridge climbs to the actual 3,192-foot summit of Coyote Mountain, which is seen some two miles north of this point.

This walk is recommended only during the cool season, since there is no shade whatsoever on the mountain. The going is easy provided you stick to the trail. If possible, carry binoculars on this trip to extend your range of vision. And, be sure to keep an eye out for that lost gold!

View of San Ysidro Mtn. from Coyote Mtn.

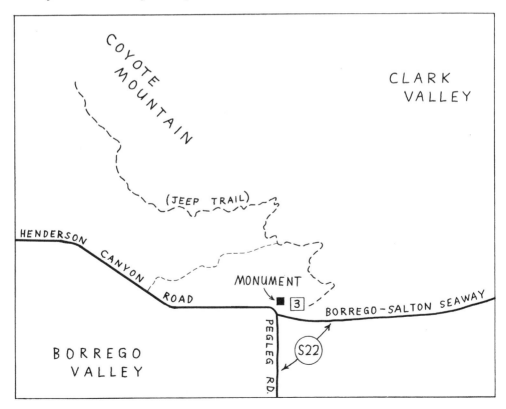

Trip 5, Trail 4 • Calcite Canyon Area

Approximate distance: 2.0 miles (1 way)
Low point (trailhead): 600 feet
High point (Calcite Mine): 1,140 feet

The Calcite Canyon area consists of a tortured landscape resulting from sandstone layers being raised, tilted and crushed against the base of an uplifted rock mass comprising the Santa Rosa Mountains. Eons of cutting and polishing by water and wind erosion have produced chaotic rock formations and steep ravines.

The event responsible for the existence of a jeep road into the very heart of this area was the discovery of large amounts of calcite crystal. During World War II, optical-grade calcite crystals were mined here for use in bomb sights. Trench mining operations left scars upon the earth, seemingly as fresh today as when they were made — a graphic illustration of the slow process by which nature heals itself using its only available remedy: erosion.

In addition to the Calcite Mine, the hiker may examine drainage patterns and the effects of flash flooding upon the washes and ravines of this area by walking through them. One such diversion is suggested for the return trip from the mine.

To reach the rough dirt parking area at the entrance to Calcite Canyon, drive east on the Borrego-Salton Seaway toward the Salton Sea. The lot is one mile west of the large microwave tower marking the east park boundary and the Imperial County line.

Follow the jeep road to the Calcite Mine as directed by the trail markers. Immediately after crossing the South Fork of Palm Wash, the road runs along a bluff overlooking Palm Wash and a small tributary. This is a good place to observe the drainage pattern below you, for the return trip will take you through these labyrinthine gorges. Dipping sharply, Calcite Road crosses the upper end of the tributary wash, then continues one-half mile up to the mining area. Here, at the road's end, numerous crystals glitter in the sunlight. Solid veins of calcite material may be found intersecting the walls of the man-made slots in the earth.

The return trip, including the diversion through Palm Wash, will allow a very different point of view. This way you will follow the narrow, confined paths of runoff from precipitation that makes only rare visits to the Santa Rosa Mountains and never remains long enough to nourish vegetation. Needless to say, these passages are the last place you would wish to be in a driving rainstorm!

Palm Wash lies only a short distance from the mine, but is inaccessible directly on foot, since it is a 30- to 50-foot vertical-walled canyon at this point. So instead, return to the aforementioned tributary wash about one-half mile down the road from the mine. Proceed "downstream" along the bottom. What begins as a moderately steep ravine cuts ever deeper into the underlying strata until, at its lower end, it becomes a deep gorge with polished sandstone walls allowing the passage of only one person at a time. No serious obstacles were found along this path at the time I explored it.

Upon reaching the jumbled boulders in Palm Wash at the mouth of the tributary, walk downstream a quarter mile to the jeep trail linking Palm Wash to the Calcite Road. Walk uphill to the top, then return to the parking area as you came.

Calcite mining area

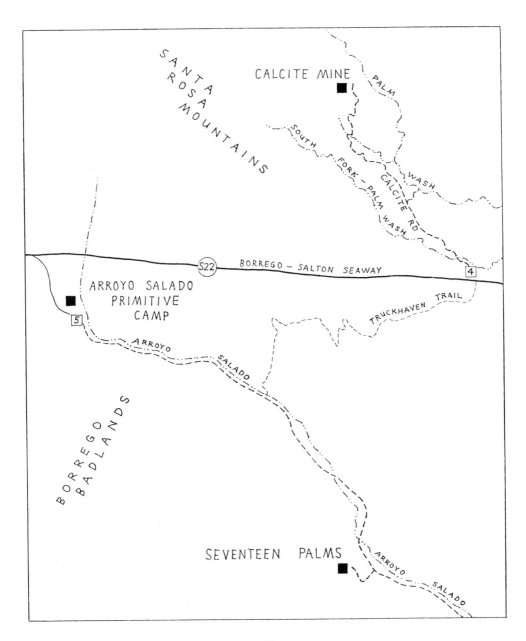

SANTA ROSA MOUNTAINS

CALCITE MINE ■

PALM

SOUTH FORK PALM WASH

CALCITE RD

WASH

S22 BORREGO – SALTON SEAWAY 4

ARROYO SALADO PRIMITIVE CAMP ■

5

ARROYO SALADO

TRUCKHAVEN TRAIL

BORREGO BADLANDS

SEVENTEEN PALMS ■

ARROYO SALADO

Trip 5, Trail 5 • Seventeen Palms Oasis

Approximate distance: 3.0 miles (1 way)
Low point (Seventeen Palms): 410 feet
High point (trailhead): 900 feet

The small oasis at Seventeen Palms on the edge of the Borrego Badlands has some long-celebrated legends associated with it. Many are the tales of lost mines and dehydrated prospectors falling swollen-tongued and gasping for the saline waters found beneath these palms. Yet, in addition to its contribution to the desert mystique, Seventeen Palms has for hundreds if not thousands of years provided the crucial element in the survival of many species of wildlife in this part of the desert.

The hike to Seventeen Palms along Arroyo Salado can be pleasant on a cool day. Carry a canteen, since the water at the oasis is not potable except in cases of extreme emergency. You may begin from Arroyo Salado primitive camp, which is located about one-half mile off the Borrego-Salton Seaway. As directed by the signs, simply follow Arroyo Salado Wash about three miles southeast to the foot trail leading to the palms. You may encounter some four-wheel drive or dune-buggy traffic along Arroyo Salado, but the last few hundred feet to the palms have been placed off-limits to motorized traffic to avoid any possible ecological damage.

At Seventeen Palms Oasis you will discover the "prospectors' post office." Decades ago, prospectors and travelers used the oasis as a point to relay messages. Today this tradition continues, and you will probably find hundreds of notes and business cards dating back several years in an old barrel beneath the palms.

Prospector's Post Office

Seventeen Palms Oasis

Trip 5, Trail 6 ● Elephant Trees Area

Approximate distance: 2.5 miles (1 way)
from Elephant Trees ranger station
Low point (parking area): 220 feet
High point (Elephant Trees): 500 feet

The harsh environment of the desert has been responsible for the evolution of many unusual species of plants and animals that have adapted successfully to arid conditions. A good example of this is the elephant tree (*Bursera microphylla*), which makes a sparse and scattered appearance in the Anza-Borrego Desert. Though common south of the border, so rare are specimens of this plant north of the border that rumors from the early 1900's of their existence in the park area were not confirmed until 1937. Today they are a recognized as a park attraction.

To reach the Elephant Trees area, drive south on Split Mountain Road — the paved road connecting with Highway 78 at Ocotillo Wells. At Elephant Trees ranger station a jeep trail leaves the main road and travels westward across a wide, sloping "bajada" toward the elephant trees which are found among the rocks near the upper end of the slope. If you wish, you may drive this jeep trail to the dirt parking lot about one mile from the ranger station. From here a nature trail loops through a dry wash and around a boulder-strewn area where the elephant trees reside.

You will recognize these trees immediately as botanical oddities. They are characterized by short stubby trunks, puffy limbs, reddish twigs and sap, green foliage and blue fruit. The largest measure some 10 feet in height and 15 feet in breadth — substantial measurements considering the absence of a permanent water supply. Like desert succulents, elephant trees are able to store water internally.

Elephant tree

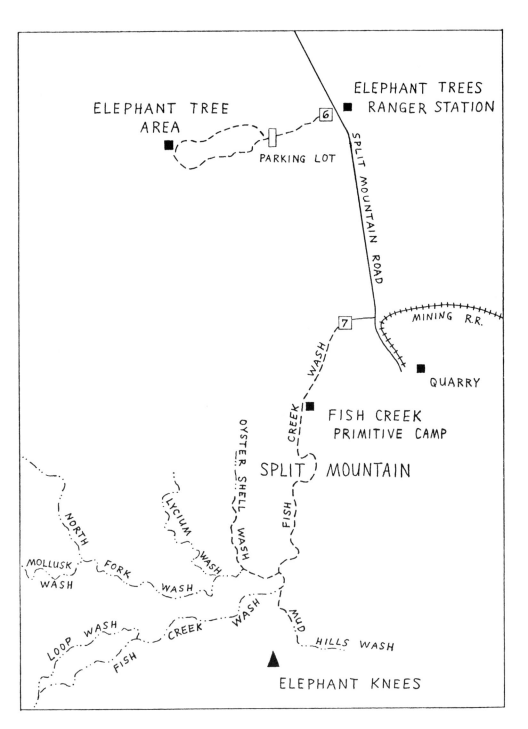

ELEPHANT TREE
AREA

ELEPHANT TREES
RANGER STATION

6

PARKING LOT

SPLIT MOUNTAIN ROAD

7

MINING R.R.

WASH

CREEK

QUARRY

FISH CREEK
PRIMITIVE CAMP

OYSTER SHELL WASH

SPLIT MOUNTAIN

FISH

LYCIUM WASH

NORTH FORK WASH

MOLLUSK WASH

WASH

LOOP WASH

FISH CREEK WASH

MUD HILLS WASH

ELEPHANT KNEES

Trip 5, Trail 7 • Split Mountain/Fish Creek Area

Approximate one-way distances from Fish Creek primitive camp: 4.5 miles to Mud Hills Wash, 5.5 miles to Oyster Shell Wash
Approximate Elevations:
Split Mountain: 400 feet
Mud Hills Wash: 550 feet
Head of Oyster Shell Wash: 1,200 feet

As if the result of some ancient Biblical catastrophe, Split Mountain appears to have been pulled apart by some almighty force on high. In reality, though, the forces have come from within the earth and have occurred in a more or less orderly fashion for the past five million years. The beginning of this period saw the present Fish Creek and Split Mountain area submerged in what was then an extension of the Gulf of California. Deep layers of sediment were deposited, and later epochs saw an increase in activity in which the land mass west of the Salton Sea was uplifted to its present elevation. Erosion has since taken its inevitable toll. It should not be forgotten, however, that catastrophic elements — flash floods and earthquakes — have played and will continue to play a major part in the area's destiny. You will be convinced of this when you see the many signs of recent geological activity at Split Mountain.

Choosing your starting point for exploration of Split Mountain and the closer tributaries of Fish Creek may well depend upon the condition of the jeep roads and the type of vehicle you drive. Either of the two destination points stated above (Mud Hills Wash and Oyster Shell Wash) are within a day's hike of the nearest paved road near Fish Creek Primitive Camp. However, one-way distances may be shortened by approximately one mile if you drive all the way to the primitive camp at the entrance to Split Mountain. Some passenger cars, as well as four-wheel drive vehicles, regularly make the journey on Fish Creek Wash through Split Mountain, but I would suggest that walking through is far more aesthetically rewarding.

The first thing you may notice upon en-

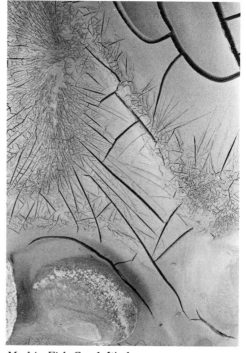

Mud in Fish Creek Wash

80

Oyster Shell Wash

tering the gorge is the series of vertical cracks and shifted strata along the west wall. Look for the fresh debris at the bottom of one of the steep ravines. This is the result of a 1968 earthquake and is reason enough to heed the ranger's advice not to camp directly beneath steep cliffs! Farther on you will notice an "anticline" of sandstone shelves bent over in an inverted U, this the result of unimaginable pressures and stresses within the earth.

Beyond Split Mountain, Fish Creek Wash splits into several forks and tributaries. When you reach the first fork, you may either continue south on Fish Creek Wash to Mud Hills Wash, or take the North Fork Wash to Oyster Shell Wash.

The mud hills, as their name suggests, are nothing but the barren and smoothly eroded remnants of the mud deposits of an ancient sea. A half-mile walk down Mud Hills Wash will provide you with a good view of the hills, which sparkle with chips of pure gypsum. Also from here you may look upon the "elephant knees" of the nearby dark-colored butte. Erosion has proceeded at varying rates upon the slope creating a Mt. Rushmore-sized sculpture. The west side of this butte contains fossil beds rich with the remains of marine organisms.

If you decide to visit Oyster Shell Wash, a tributary of the North Fork of Fish Creek Wash, hike up beyond the end of the jeep trail. Here you will find water-polished sandstone walls and shallow depressions sometimes filled with water. Keep your eyes open for the oyster shell remnants that are commonly found in this area.

If you decide to visit both Mud Hills and Oyster Shell Wash, the total round trip distance would be about 13 miles from the paved road (or 11 miles from the primitive camp). Be sure to allow plenty of time to explore the Fish Creek area — you never know what curiosities may draw you away from the beaten path.

Mud Hills Wash

Entrance to Split Mountain

Trip 5, Trail 8 ● Pedro Fages Trail

Approximate distance: 9.0 miles (1 way)
Low point (Mason Valley): 2,310 feet
High point (near Cuyamaca Reservoir):
4,790 feet

In 1772, Pedro Fages started east from San Diego in pursuit of deserters from the presidio. His initial travels took him straight into the unknown interior mountains and deserts of present-day San Diego County, and resulted in the discovery of two important land routes through the Anza-Borrego Desert. Fages and his men made their way down to the desert on an Indian trail through Oriflamme Canyon, the first official entry into the Colorado Desert by the Spaniards. Fages left the desert by a northern passage through Coyote Canyon, which was rediscovered two years later by Anza and his party of settlers.

Today a portion of the California Riding and Hiking Trail from Cuyamaca Lake in the Cuyamaca Mountains to Mason Valley in the Anza-Borrego Desert roughly follows Fages' historical descent through Oriflamme Canyon. This nine-mile segment, which ties together existing dirt roads and jeep trails, is suitable for a one-way day hike if transportation is arranged at both ends. If you prefer the downhill direction, the 2,400-foot descent should take only 3 to 5 hours; in the meantime, your compatriots can make the journey by car through Julian and Banner to the pre-arranged rendezvous point in the desert. While browsing in Julian, of course, they should not forget to pick up plenty of cold apple cider for the hot and thirsty hikers arriving at the end of the trail!

Topside, the best place to park is at the Pedro Fages monument on Highway S1 near the junction of Highway 79. From here hikers walk 300 yards west on the highway to the cattle guard that marks the intersection of the California Riding and Hiking Trail and the highway. Follow the trail northward about two miles from the road to the point where the Riding and Hiking Trail splits into two branches; take the right-hand fork which turns eastward toward Borrego Springs as indicated by the sign. The left fork continues northward to Warner Springs and the San Jacinto Mountains beyond.

A moderately steep descent, then a level stretch precedes the sharp drop to the bottom of Oriflamme Canyon. At the mouth of the canyon, the trail emerges upon the gentle terrain of Mason Valley, and cacti appear in ever increasing numbers.

The parking area in lower Box Canyon (west of the historical monument) along Highway S2 is a possible rendezvous point at the desert end of the trail. The California Riding and Hiking Trail intersects the highway only a half-mile from here, and continues eastward along the south side of the road.

In the course of the journey, you will cross a number of private land-holdings, so make certain to close the unlocked gates behind you. In addition to the horsemen you'll see on the trail, you might encounter some four-wheel drive or motorcycle traffic in some sections.

Teddy-Bear Cholla Cactus

Beehives in Mason Valley

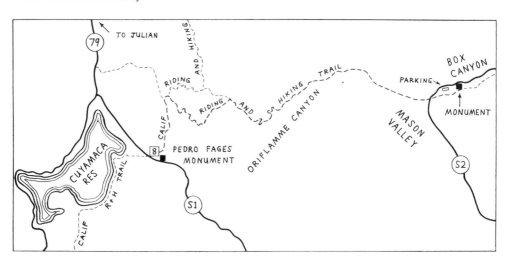

Trip 5, Trail 9 ● Moonlight Canyon Trail

Approximate distance: 1.5 miles round trip
Low point (trailhead): 1,310 feet
High point: 1,650 feet

To me, sunrise on the desert seems to impart a sense of absolute quiet and stillness. The sun cautiously peeps over the eastern horizon and silent shadows recede in an age-old ritual of rebirth. For a brief hour or two, cool air from the previous night clings to the ground, and the true colors of rock and minerals are as yet undisguised by the harsh glare of the midday sun.

The Moonlight Canyon Trail is one that is best suited to early morning exploration. You will find it at Agua Caliente Springs County Park, a camping area located next to the "hot water" springs off County Highway S2. Be sure to bring a bathing suit, so that you may enjoy a dip in the tepid waters of the spring-fed therapeutic pool before or after the hike.

The trail is well-marked from the beginning at campsite 82 as it enters Moonlight Canyon, climbs up and over a saddle and drops back down to the campgrounds. In the stillness of the morning you can sense the presence of moisture just before you reach some small seeps at the bottom of the canyon. On the high point of the trail, you'll be treated to a fine view of the Vallecito Mountains to the north. Morning or late afternoon sunlight shines low and obliquely across the face of these mountains creating a classic desert panorama.

Drop by Agua Caliente Springs sometime for a short walk and a refreshing dip in the pool.

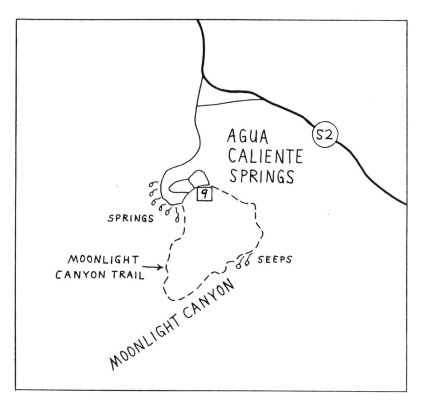

AGUA CALIENTE SPRINGS

S2

9

SPRINGS

MOONLIGHT CANYON TRAIL

SEEPS

MOONLIGHT CANYON

Vallecito Mountains

Trip 5, Trail 10 • Mountain Palm Springs

Approximate distance: 1.0 mile (1 way) to Palm Bowl Grove, 1.5 miles (1 way) to Torote Bowl
Low point (trailhead): 760 feet
High point (Torote Bowl): 1,320 feet

The Mountain Palm Springs area in the southern half of the park is another example of palm oases in the midst of desolation. Though not as spectacular as Borrego Palm Canyon to the north, this area has nevertheless suffered far less from trampling by human footsteps, and it remains essentially in a pristine state. Several palm groves, some of them supplied by plentiful amounts of water, are distributed in three branch canyons.

You may begin your exploration of this area from Mountain Palm Springs primitive camp, located one-half mile off County S2 roughly two miles north of Bow Willow Campground. If you follow the north wash, signs will direct you to North Grove, Surprise Canyon Grove, and Palm Bowl Grove. Of these, Palm Bowl has the greatest number of palm trees, but Surprise Canyon Grove seems to have the best above-ground water supply.

Following the south fork trail will take you past Pygmy Grove to Southwest Grove and its waterhole. A catch-basin lined with rocks has been built here to provide a good water source for the local wildlife which, aside from birds, usually consists of coyotes, jackrabbits, and bighorn sheep. For a look at some elephant trees in the vicinity, follow the signs from Southwest Grove to Torote Bowl. Here on a rocky hillside you will find that botanical oddity known as "torote" to the Mexicans — elephant trees to us.

Aside from a brief visit to the waterholes, it is recommended that you don't camp, picnic or linger near them for long periods of time. Many animals require at least one drink of water per day, but will forego this if people are present. Also one word of caution — probe for rattlesnakes if you tramp through the fallen palm fronds and underbrush in the palm groves.

Pygmy Palms

88

Variety of vegetation at Mountain Palm Springs

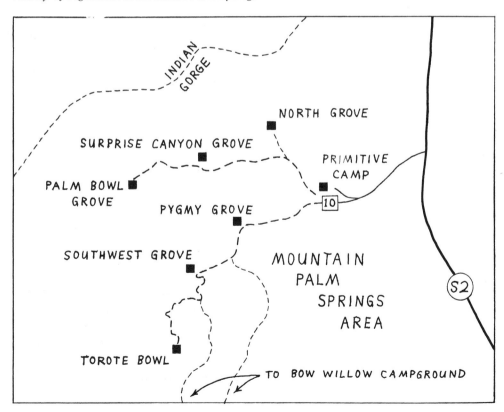

INDIAN GORGE

NORTH GROVE

SURPRISE CANYON GROVE

PRIMITIVE CAMP

PALM BOWL GROVE

PYGMY GROVE

10

SOUTHWEST GROVE

MOUNTAIN PALM SPRINGS AREA

S2

TOROTE BOWL

TO BOW WILLOW CAMPGROUND

Palms at Southwest Grove – Mountain Palm Spring

Trip 5, Trail 11 ● Bow Willow Canyon-Rockhouse Canyon Trail

Approximate distance: 7.0 miles round trip
Low point (trailhead): 1,020 feet
High point: 1,740 feet

Fill up your canteens for this one. You'll tread many a mile of jagged, rocky terrain utterly devoid of water. Also advisable are sturdy boots and long pants to protect you against the desert agave and cholla cactus which grow in abundance here.

Begin at Bow Willow Campground, located two miles west of Highway S2 down a good road of hard-packed sand. Park here and walk past the seasonal ranger station and developed campsites to a point nearly one-half mile beyond, where a small arroyo, a tributary of Bow Willow Canyon, enters from the south. Begin the loop portion of this trip from here.

Less than one-half mile up the arroyo is a single young palm tree, with its dead fronds matted snugly against the lower half of the trunk. Here, then, is a palm canyon with only one palm tree. A steep climb through an obstacle course of granite boulders is next. The going is easy at the top where a smooth, wide wash leads gently upward to a plateau area of broken rock formations and cactus gardens. It's easy to lose the trail at this point, so watch carefully for the rock cairns and brown and yellow trail markers. Don't rely upon the footprints to guide your way — they can lead you astray. At least one cairn should be visible ahead from any point on the trail.

At Rockhouse Canyon, the trail drops down to join an abandoned jeep trail leading to the namesake of the canyon — an old rock shelter once used by cattlemen. You'll find it nestled against the mountains on the south side of the canyon. If the midday sun beats

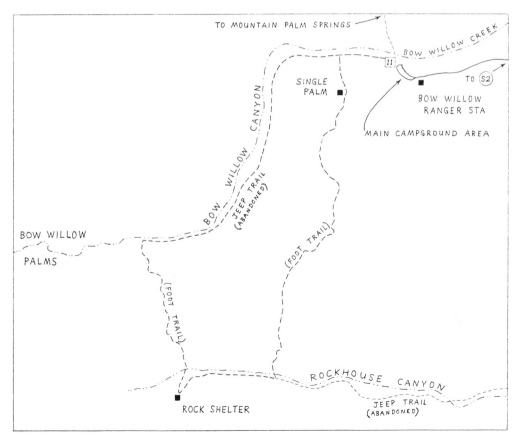

91

down unmercifully, this is a cool spot for a rest or a picnic. When the water table is "up," you may find surface water in the ravine behind the rock house.

From the rock house, the hiking trail heads directly north straight over a low pass in the divide between Rockhouse and Bow Willow canyons. Once over the summit, you drop quickly to the floor of Bow Willow Canyon. If your wish is to do further exploring, try Bow Willow Palms; make the side trip to the point 1½ miles west and just off our map, where the canyon divides. Both branches have palms, but the left (south) fork carries a stream of water that flows almost year round.

If heading for home is your inclination by now, just make the easy stroll down the jeep road in Bow Willow Canyon to return to the starting point. Don't miss the elephant trees clinging to the canyon wall, high and to your right.

Old Rock House – Bow Willow-Rockhouse Canyon Trail

Trip 5, Trail 12 • Canyon Sin Nombre

Approximate distance: 2.5 miles (1 way)
Low point (Canyon Sin Nombre): 760 feet
High point (trailhead): 1,210 feet

Nowhere else in the desert will you find the raw erosive power of flash flooding better illustrated than in the badlands. Stripped of vegetation and acted upon by the opposing forces of geologic uplift and gravity-induced drainage, the sandstone and mud cliffs of the badlands offer mute testimony of their creation.

The Carrizo Badlands is one such area of the Anza-Borrego Desert that is easily accessible to hikers and four-wheel drive vehicles. The jeep trail to Canyon Sin Nombre — Canyon without a Name — begins on County Highway S2 three miles south of the entrance to Bow Willow Campground. You may park off the highway here, but don't attempt to drive on the Canyon Sin Nombre jeep trail in a passenger car. The trail is in soft sand and heads immediately downhill toward the canyon. Barrel cacti dot the flats along the trail and the slopes of the nearby mountains, some growing to heights of five feet.

A mile from the starting point, the trail enters the canyon. Inside nothing but jagged rock towers on all sides. The solid rock is later replaced by sandstone and mud with chaotic patterns and colors etched into the canyon walls.

When the canyon begins to widen, follow the smooth, convoluted mud walls on the west side. Look for the jeep trail that leaves the main path to enter the vertical-walled tributary canyon on the left. Follow this trail to the end, then (for the sure-footed only) continue climbing up the gorge as it narrows to a veritable crevasse — a "fat man's misery" situation.

My impression at this point was feeling as though I was in a subterranean passageway surrounded by nothing but sand and dried mud, groping toward an uncertain destination. The destination, as it turned out, was surprising: the top of the cliffs overlooking Canyon Sin Nombre. Nature had provided an easy route.

Sandstone and Mudwalled Gorge

The scene here is total desolation. In the absence of wind, there is also the absence of sound. On clear days perspective seems warped, so that objects beyond close range appear pasted onto the horizon, as in a Hollywood movie set. Let your mind wander back in time, reversing the effects of erosion, and imagine how this land appeared in prehistoric times.

Let your imagination take wing, but don't lose track of your footsteps! There is only one easy way to return to Canyon Sin Nombre — the way you came.

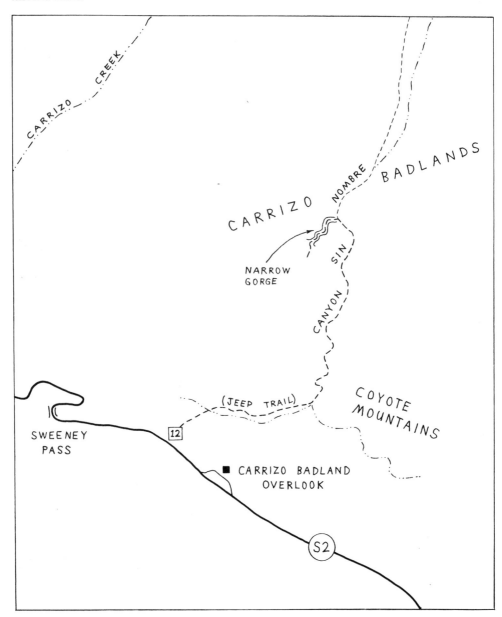

Sandstone Formations in Canyon Sin Nombre

Some additional areas of the Anza-Borrego Desert State Park that are not included in the above sections are worth mentioning:

Coyote Canyon and its major western tributaries (Alder, Salvador, Sheep, Cougar, and Indian canyons) are accessible by jeep trail northwest from Borrego Valley. The creek in the canyon is the only stream in the park that flows year-round. The best spots along the creek are Middle Willows and Lower Willows/Santa Catarina Spring, both sporting luxuriant riparian vegetation.

The Natural Rock Tanks in Smoke Tree Canyon may be approached by way of an unmarked foot trail beginning near the mouth of Palo Verde Canyon. This obscure trail is shown on the U.S.G.S. 7.5-minute topographic map "Fonts Point." The intersection of Palo Verde Wash and Borrego-Salton Seaway (County S22) is a good place to start.

The Pinyon Mountain jeep trail leaves Highway S2 at the south end of Earthquake Valley, and runs eastward to a broad saddle in the heart of the Vallecito and Pinyon mountains. About two miles south of this saddle is pinyon pine-studded Whale Peak, probably the most interesting peak to climb in the park. Use the U.S.G.S. 7.5 minute "Whale Peak" map to help plan a route to the top.

From the Little Pass primitive camp in Blair Valley you may follow a dirt road, then a hiking trail, to the Indian pictographs in Smuggler Canyon. A spur road and trail leads to the mountaintop site of "Yaquitepec," the hand-built adobe home in which desert writer Marshal South and his poetess wife, Tanya, and children lived in seclusion in the 1930's and 40's.

Exploration of the Bow Willow Palms, found at the remote upper end of Bow Willow Canyon and in some of its tributaries, is a strenuous undertaking for experienced hikers, but very rewarding.

The interior portions of the Borrego Badlands and the Carrizo Badlands contain mazes of jeep trails suitable for off-road vehicles. The jeep routes in the Carrizo Badlands are often little-traveled and serve as fine routes for hiking.

Carrizo Gorge and its palm-studded tributaries can be reached by sandy jeep tracks south from Highway S2 near Bow Willow Campground. The Carrizo Palms, along with the Dos Cabezas and Mortero Palms areas, may be reached by a number of dirt roads and jeep trails south from Highway S2 and in the area west of the town of Ocotillo.

U.S.G.S. topographic maps are a handy reference for all areas described in this book. They are sold through retail map shops and outdoor shops throughout Southern California or you can purchase them directly from the U.S. Government. Write to U.S. Geological Survey, Box 25286 Federal Center, Denver, CO 80225 for a free index map of California.

Maps of the Cleveland National Forest and the various state and county parks covered in this book are also available at ranger stations and park offices. A set of black-and-white reproductions of eight U.S.G.S. 15-minute topographic maps covering all of the Anza-Borrego area in fair detail is available at the Anza-Borrego Desert State Park Visitor Center in Borrego Springs.

About the Author

Jerry Schad, a fifth-generation Californian, has resided in San Diego County since 1972. Seldom seen without a camera, he likes to spend weekends bicycling and hiking the backcountry roads and trails of San Diego County. Weekdays he teaches astronomy and physics at San Diego area community colleges.

Editor, Thomas K. Worcester